The Year's Work in Medievalism

The Year's Work in Medievalism

Edited by E. L. Risden

XXVI
2011

WIPF & STOCK · Eugene, Oregon

THE YEAR'S WORK IN MEDIEVALISM

Copyright © 2012 Edward Risden, Series Editor. All rights reserved. Except for brief quotations in critical publications or reviews, no part of this book may be reproduced in any manner without prior written permission from the publisher. Write: Permissions, Wipf and Stock Publishers, 199 W. 8th Ave., Suite 3, Eugene, OR 97401.

Wipf & Stock
An Imprint of Wipf and Stock Publishers
199 W. 8th Ave., Suite 3
Eugene, OR 97401
www.wipfandstock.com

ISBN 13: 978-1-62032-303-8
Manufactured in the U.S.A.

The Year's Work in Medievalism, volume XXVI, is based upon but not restricted to the 2011 proceedings of the annual International Conference on Medievalism, organized by the Director of Conferences for the International Society for the Study of Medievalism.

The 2011 volume is indexed in The Modern Language Association International Bibliography.

Copyright International Society for the Study of Medievalism 2011

All rights reserved. Except as permitted under current legislation, no part of this work may be photocopied, stored in a retrieval system, published, transmitted, or reproduced in any form or by any means without prior permission of the copyright owner.

The Year's Work in Medievalism is an imprint of Studies in Medievalism. For inquiries, write E. L. Risden, Editor, The Year's Work in Medievalism, Department of English, St. Norbert College, 100 Grant St., De Pere, WI 54115.

Contents

Introductory Letter from the Editor vii
     E. L. Risden

Recollections of Medievalism 1
     Gwendolyn Morgan

Them Philologists: Philological Practices and Their Discontents
         from Nietzsche to Cerquiglini 4
     Richard Utz

Really Ancient Druids in British Medievalist Drama 13
     Clare Simmons

Neomedievalisms in Tom Phillips' *Commedia* Illustrations 27
     Karl Fugelso

Some Contributions to Middle-earth Lexicography:
         Hapax Legomena in *The Lord of the Rings* 36
     Jason Fisher

The World of Warcraft: A Medievalist Perspective 49
     Simon Roffey

Arthur, Beowulf, Robin Hood, and Hollywood's Desire for Origins 66
     William Hodapp

The Arthurian Landscapes of Guy Gavriel Kay 90
     M. J. Toswell

Introductory Letter from the Editor

I'd like to begin my first number of *The Year's Work in Medievalism* by thanking Gwendolyn Morgan for her distinguished tenure as editor of the journal: please see her essay beginning this volume, and I dedicate the volume to her in thanks from all of us who have read and contributed over those years.

I think you'll enjoy, in addition, essays by contributors many of whose names you'll find familiar from *Year's Work* or from scholarship in medievalism generally: Richard Utz, Clare Simmons, Karl Fugelso, Jason Fisher, Simon Roffey, William Hodapp, and Jane Toswell. I hope we will be able to continue the tradition of featuring both practiced (not to say *older*) scholars and those new to the field as well.

While *YWiM* began largely as a proceedings, it has come to stand on its own feet as a fully refereed journal, so I offer my thanks and appreciation to the readers who spent irreplaceable work (and sometimes leisure) time responding to the essays: journals wouldn't be proper journals without you.

One particular aim I have for our journal is to increase its circulation and readership: the field of medievalism continues to broaden its interests and expand its number of inheritors, so if you read *YWiM* regularly, please consider subscribing or asking your institution to subscribe. Wipf and Stock do a fine job of producing an appealing and affordable print product, and we should take advantage of their expertise and do more to circulate copies among our growing tribe and provide a professional forum to encourage scholarly pursuits.

For those readers interested in contributing, please remember that we are an annual and work with the most limited staff: the readers and me. You can speed the process of review by following the journal format explicitly (Chicago Manual of Style with footnotes) and submitting essays by the first of August for the following year's number (e.g., please send by August 1, 2012, for the 2013 number). While I won't adhere to that

Introductory Letter from the Editor

date as a strict deadline, you'll make my job easier and allow for earlier release of the next number by attending to it. Please send documents as Word files, preferably .doc format, until you hear otherwise from me: my computer software remains a bit behind the times. Please think of *YWiM* (remember, too, that we deal strictly with medievalism as our subject matter) as an outlet for shorter articles (in the 3000-4000 word range); if you have longer articles (say 8000 words or longer), please send them to Karl Fugelso at Towson State University for consideration for *Studies in Medievalism*. Prof. Fugelso often edits themed volumes as well, so please keep apprised of the plans for the upcoming issues. If you have a conference paper that you'd like to submit, please brush and polish it first and conform it to the requested format: many of our *YWiM* essays begin as papers at the annual International Society for the Study of Medievalism conference, but readers and editors appreciate receiving text ready for a print rather than listening audience. Best wishes to readers and contributors alike, and I look forward to hearing from you and working with you. I hope this is the beginning of a beautiful friendship.

Thanks to Dr. Jeff Frick, Dean and Academic Vice President of St. Norbert College, for financial support for this volume.

—E. L. Risden,
Professor of English,
St. Norbert College edward.risden@snc.edu

Recollections of Medievalism

Gwendolyn Morgan, Montana State University

WHEN THE CURRENT EDITOR suggested I write a reflective essay on my twenty-two years of association with the International Society for the Study of Medievalism, I initially thought to chronicle the development of *The Year's Work in Medievalism*, of which I was general (and frequently issue) editor for eleven years. Yet he saved both me and any readers from obligatory boredom when he suggested I "have fun with it." Yes! But how, I wondered, is that possible? Editing a journal is not exactly fun. No, but as the longest-standing current member (excepting the co-founder) of ISSM (The International Society for the Study of Medievalism), vice-president for ten years, and organizer of conferences for fifteen, I have also become the unofficial keeper of conference lore. So here goes.

Notice we are an international organization. The year before I allied myself with ISSM, the annual conference was in Germany, and in 2010 in the Netherlands (the only meeting I have missed in twenty-two years), but I can't speak to either of them. However, Fredericton, Canada has distinguished itself not only as the "conference of food" for its elegant and delectable luncheons and banquet, but as the birthplace of the "Medieval Moorish Maidens," an attempt by three of us to write (without communication in a Bridges of Madison County sort of way) the tale of six tenth-century dancing girls in six chapters, employing all linguistic and poetic styles from the English and French Middle Ages. The intent was to have the "manuscript" discovered a barn loft in southern Ontario, as was the most authentic portrait of Shakespeare, then to present the discovery at Kalamazoo. Sadly, our project never got off the ground: even in Old English style alliterative verse, orange is a difficult word to work with. Then there were the Canterbury Cops, who attempted to arrest an association member (who shall remain nameless) for leading a tour group without license. It wasn't his fault, really: he was merely waxing eloquent in the cathedral in a loud sort of way, and other people starting following us. To lovely London, Ontario, we owe the current name of the organization, and the Lost in Leeds crew will recall our conference host moved to the United States shortly before we arrived at his former institution for the annual meeting.

But usually we stay at home in the United States. Really, it's frequently more interesting, as anyone who recalls our Tampa meeting invasion by a coven of witches will agree. And we ourselves are not blameless for our medieval theater of the absurd. Why, recently in Albuquerque, many of us refused to surrender our lunch tickets to the servers because they were so pretty (the tickets, that is), and in Cedar Falls, a colleague of our host who was playing mini-bus chauffeur to the banquet locked us and himself out of our bus during a sleet storm (we took a taxi). Yet in Iowa, at least we ate. In Saint Louis, the graduate student servers at the banquet over-indulged, and the last table went hungry, but the host did provide us a supply of free wine adequate to make us forget. Holland, Michigan, brought us our current President, whose panel of two papers had an audience of two (the daughter of the other speaker and the moderator, me). Obviously, I did well to convince him to join us again next year. It was also the birth place of the Prose Gwendolyn by Bill Calin (which also was never written). The best drama, however, was the Albany Absurdity, a fiasco in which, after escaping from the home of a mad dentist where costumed, life-size dummies of Camelot's finest dominated the living room and original family heraldry and other curios of medievalism fashioned from dental plaster decorated the walls, we crammed seven people into a compact car and tore through red lights attempting to elude our pursuer. Oh yes, the "short walk" to campus from the hotel there turned out to be seven miles. Then there are things beyond our control: the two hurricanes, for example.

Ah, I do love our conferences!

Nonetheless, ISSM meetings have been memorable intellectual feasts as well. Our keynote speakers have been luminaries: Norman Cantor, Terry Jones, Ronald Hutton, Verlyn Fleiger, for example. Our panels range from literature and theater to musicology and art history, to graphic novels, popular film, and video games. Most spectacular, though, are our participants, who brave hurricanes, post-911 security issues, and the inconvenience of flights from nowhere to (frequently) nowhere, to share projects and discoveries and the pure joy of our subject. Medievalism unites scholars from all disciplines and specialists in all periods, and

I, for one, am immeasurably enriched by it. And I have seen medievalism develop from Leslie Workman's voice crying in the wilderness to a mainstream focus in the academy.

Which leads me to my last (obligatory but also satisfying) observation: the growth of *The Year's Work in Medievalism*. Published sporadically until 1999, and self-published by Studies in Medievalism until 2002, the *Year's Work* is now a substantial annual journal copyrighted by ISSN and published by Wipf and Stock in standard format. It has gone from a conference proceedings to peer-reviewed submissions, from at times suffering from an insufficient number of quality manuscripts to being sought out as a venue. It is a voice and a source, drawing attention from publishers and academic institutions alike. A quarter of a century ago, Leslie Workman insisted it would ultimately become the most important resource in the field, and I can say with confidence that it is on its way.

Them Philologists

Philological Practices and Their Discontents from Nietzsche to Cerquiglini

Richard Utz, Western Michigan University

IN 1954 HOLLYWOOD PRODUCED the blockbuster *Them*, which presented a scenario in which an uncontrolled atomic explosion in the American south-west had led to the growth of gigantic mutant ants who threatened to destroy humanity. As in other Cold War monster movies, the ants, insects often associated with the anti-individualistic societies of Japan, China, or Nazi Germany, were depicted as *Them*, the evil, inhuman, and completely "other," whereas civilization and its champions were warm-blooded U.S. citizens and their children, who would in the end manage to defend all of Western civilization against a threatening Asia that, like an ever-reproducing colony of soulless worker ants, was hell-bent on machine-like procreation and violent colonization and extermination.[1]

    Fascinatingly, the othering of one's enemy in Cold War cinema as diligent, but unnaturally overwhelming, mechanistic, and inhuman is also a central feature of the widespread opposition to philological practices and practitioners from the second half of the nineteenth century through the present. Consider, if you will, Henry Sweet's exasperated complaint in 1885 about how "the historical study of English" had been "rapidly annexed" by "swarms of young program-mongers" turned out every year by the German universities, "so thoroughly trained in all the mechanical details of what may be called 'parasite philology' that no English dilettante can hope to compete with them– except by Germanizing

---

    1. One of the best-known comparisons of Nazi Germany and the social life of ants is T. H. White's *The Once and Future King* (London: Collins, 1958) and *The Book of Merlyn* (written 1941; published Austin and London: University of Texas Press, 1977).

himself and losing all hope of his nationality," all the consequence "of our own neglect, and of the unhealthy over-production of the German universities."² Twenty-nine years later, at the eve of World War I, British antipathy to an allegedly German philology had become even more virulent. Declaring their solidarity with their government's goals for the war against Germany, fifty-two nationally-known writers and critics, including H. Granville Barker, J.M. Barrie, G.K. Chesterton, Arthur Conan Doyle, H. Rider Haggard, Thomas Hardy, Rudyard Kipling, Henry Newbolt, Arthur Quiller-Couch, and G.M. Trevelyan, defined the military conflict as the ineluctable continuation of an existing intellectual altercation that would render, in the words of Basil Willey, English studies "an autonomous discipline" free from "the alien yoke of Teutonic philology."³ For Ezra Pound, an English philology was "evil, a perversion," and intimately linked with the militaristic mentality of the German "Junker." The educational method behind philology, Pound stated,

> holds up an ideal of "scholarship," not an ideal of humanity. It says in effect: you are to acquire knowledge in order that knowledge may be acquired. Metaphorically, you are to build up a dam'd and useless pyramid which will be no use to you or anyone else, but which will serve as a "monument". To this end you are to sacrifice your mind and vitality. [. . .] This is [. . .] the symptom of the disease; it is all one with the idea that the man is the slave of the State, the "unit", the piece of the machine.⁴

Sweet's and Pound's statements share an overwhelming anti-German sentiment, and German philologists had in fact done what they could in the forty years leading up to World War I to propagate philological practices as a national virtue at which they outshone the scholars in any other country. Thus, and despite the opposition of J.R.R. Tolkien, who proclaimed that philology was neither "a purely German invention" nor

---

2. Henry Sweet, ed., *The Oldest English Texts* (London: EETS, 1885), vii.

3. Basil Willey, *Cambridge and Other Memories, 1920–1953* (London: Chatto and Windus, 1964), 24.

4. Ezra Pound, "Provincialism the Enemy," in *Ezra Pound. Selected Prose 1909–1965*, ed. William Cookson (London: New Directions, 1973), 161–62. Pound's essay originally appeared in the journal *New Age* on 12 July 1917. On the consequences of World War I on the practices and nomenclature of the academic study of English in Britain and Germany, see Richard Utz, "*Englische Philologie* vs. English Studies: A Foundational Conflict," in *Das Potential europäischer Philologien. Geschichte, Leistung, Funktion*, ed. Christoph König (Göttingen: Wallstein, 2009), 34–44.

something "that the late war was fought to end," but rather an "essential piece of apparatus [. . .] as universal as is the use of language," the 1922 *Newbolt Report* on *The Position of English in the Educational System of England* publicly denounced philology as an alien practice that busied itself with "hypothetical sound-shiftings in the primeval German forests" instead of enabling students "to read our early literature with understanding and enjoyment" and to appreciate "the humane and aesthetic significance of language as the expression of thought."[5]

In order to extricate ourselves from the druidical mist of late nineteenth- and early twentieth-century nationalism, let me move forward in time to what should count as a post-national critique of philology, Bernard Cerquiglini's 1989 *Éloge de la variante: Histoire Critique de la philologie*, which helped inspire the North American movement known as the "New Philology" and/or the "New Medievalism." In the introduction to his *essai*, Cerquiglini states, here in Betsy Wing's translation: "At the dawn of the nineteenth century, extremely diverse phenomena of order, nature, and evolution all seemed to converge, forming a coherent semantics connected with the practice and study of texts. Philology is the most significant expression of this coherence."[6]

Cerquiglini then continues to point out the various elements that contributed to what he summarizes as "textuary modernity," the foundation of philology:

1) Historical positivism, which displays a semi-religious trust in the

---

5. J. R. R. Tolkien, "Philology: General Works," in the *Year's Work in English Studies* 4 (1923), 20–37, here 36–37. The second quote is by Sir Walter Raleigh (1861–1922), Chair of English at Oxford, whose opinion, together with those of other experts, is cited in what is commonly referred to as the *Newbolt Report* because it was produced and published under the supervision of Sir Henry Newbolt; the document's full title is: *The Teaching of English in England, Being the Report of the Departmental Committee Appointed by the president of the Board of Education to Inquire into the Position of English in the Educational System of England* (London, HMSO, 1921).

6. *In Praise of the Variant. A Critical History of Philology*, trans. Betsy Wing (Baltimore: Johns Hopkins University Press, 1999), xiv. The French original, *Éloge de la variante. Histoire critique de la philologie*, was published by Éditions du Seuil in 1989. There are, I should admit, some potential nationalist resonances in the strong French opposition to German(ic) philology. They begin with Joseph Bédier, the warrior scholar at the Collège de France, one of Cerquiglini's points of reference for his critical history of the subject. Michelle Warren, in *Creole Medievalism. Colonial France and Joseph Bédier's Middle Ages* (Minneapolis: University of Minnesota Press, 2011), has recently shown Bédier's nationalist academic practice as shaped by unique "Réunionnais migrant echoes" (xi).

factual nature of texts and wants to apply critical reflection only to such reliable texts;

2) A printing industry that reaches a mechanized state in which the author exercises complete control over faithful copy in order to avoid the alteration and variance that characterize pre-modern textual reproduction;

3) A legal situation in which any text belonged to the person who conceived it, in which in Foucault's words any given text became a genitive, i.e., "work of" a person.

Thus, according to Cerquiglini, a modern science was anachronistically thrust upon pre-modern texts, preferring the perfect facsimile to individual editing, correcting scribal indeterminacy and grammatical variance, and reconstituting legal textual paternity. These efforts demanded "an insane amount of erudition" (page 50) by scholars whom Cerquiglini likens to the Greek figure of Procrustes, the bandit smith who would either stretch or cut off his prisoners' legs to make them fit his arbitrary standard of ideal length, a mid-sized iron bed.[7] The entire arsenal of philology, all meant to obliterate the sin of scholarly subjectivity (*recensio, emendatio, stemma codicum*, critical apparatus) reveals itself as "a bourgeois, paternalist, and hygienist system" of forced epistemological unity about the family: "it cherishes filiation, tracks down adulterers, and is afraid of contamination. It is thought based on what is wrong (the variant being a form of deviant behavior) [...].["8]

Cerquiglini's outspoken opposition to modernist philology, while free from the national animosity that informs Sweet and Pound, repeats the known accusations against philological practices: its machine-like, mechanized drive toward conformity and normativity as well as its insane and cruel inhumanity. It appears, then, that scholars like Cerquiglini, and in his wake the New Philologists, object mainly to philology's modernist and scientific features, its attempt at eliminating the subjective, artistic, and violently anti-normative, i.e., the human element in literary and textual creation, a dichotomy Friedrich Nietzsche had attempted to heal in his own idiosyncratic response to academic work. Nietzsche, who had his Prussian citizenship annulled and remained stateless for the rest of his

---

[7]. The quote is from *In Praise of the Variant*, page 50. Chapter 2 of the monograph is entitled: "Mr. Procrustes, Philologist."

[8]. *In Praise of the Variant*, 49.

life, preferring to see himself as "a good European" rather than a citizen of any one country, shares with Cerquiglini a kind of post-nationalist stance. In his 1869 inaugural address as Professor of Classical Philology at the University of Basel, he produced one of his first programmatic definitions of philology:[9]

> We have to admit that, in all honesty, Philology is scrounged together from several sciences, concocted like a magic potion out of the strangest liquors, ores, and bones. It even contains an artistic and aesthetically and ethically grounded imperatival element, one that stands in opposition to purely scientific practice. It is just as much a piece of History as it is a Natural Science or Aesthetics: Part of History because it wants to comprehend the manifestations of specific national features in ever-new images, to understand the guiding principles within the quickly-changing fugue of events; part of the Natural Sciences because it wants to investigate the deepest human instinct, the instinct of language; and part of Aesthetics, finally, because it wants to construct out of a series of antiquities the so-called "Classical" Antiquity and intends to excavate an obscured ideal world and to hold up the mirror of a Classical and Eternally Perfect world to the contemporary world. The reason why these thoroughly diverse scientific and aesthetic/ethical instincts united under a common umbrella term can [. . .] be explained by the fact that philology has always also been a form of pedagogical practice. This pedagogical practice demanded that a selection of the pedagogically and educationally valuable elements be made. Thus, under the pressure of this necessity, has evolved the academic temper we call Philology.[10]

Niezsche continues his description of philology by creating a composite picture of the area's two groups of "omnipresent enemies," those who deride philologists as innocuous "moles" who "practice inhaling dust *ex professo*" and those who fear the strength of the noble Hellenistic ideal and its criticism of contemporary "barbarity." Beyond these groups, he

---

9. His appointment in Switzerland, a country relatively uninvolved in the storm clouds that would lead to the Franco-Prussian War and WW I, may be the reason for his pre-/post-national stance in this speech.

10. "Homer und die classische Philologie," in Friedrich Nietzsche, *Nachgelassene Werke. Aus den Jahren 1869–1872* (Leipzig: C. G. Neumann, 1903), 1–24, here 1–2. This translation of Nietzsche's speech is my own. I retain the caps for the various disciplines and subdisciplines in Nietzsche's original because they suggest their quality as personified abstractions (pretty much what Nietzsche calls "Aggregatszustand").

sees philologists as their own worst enemies, jealously fighting against each other ("gegenseitige Eifersüchtigkeiten") about priority and authority in their fields ("unnützer Rangstreit").[11]

The proverbial defense of the idealized simple and noble Greek aside, Nietzsche's definition of philology shows him cognizant of his own area of specialty as an "inorganic" and "multifacetted" signifier or "magic potion" that consists of strange "liquors, ores, and bones," i.e., historicism, ethics, and aesthetics. He sees the exact mix of this alchemical potion as decided by the pedagogical application each historical period or, by extension, national tradition, making philology a discipline that exists in its various nineteenth-century forms because of the very exigencies a century or nation impresses upon it. In its disarming simplicity, Nietzsche's inaugural speech helps us understand why philology would, in Germany, transform into a weapon the unified nation state would wield in its desire to build up the most streamlined and effective educational system and why, in the Anglo-Saxon world, philology would be tempered or resisted by those who thought that the study of historical texts should, in the words of Arthur Quiller-Couch, be more than "an abstract Science, to which exact definitions can be applied. It is an Art rather, the success of which depends on personal persuasiveness, on the author's skill to give as on ours to receive."[12] Nietzsche is not worried about the "pedantic tendencies" of philology that persuaded H. M. Chadwick, in the 1930s, to attach Anglo-Saxon Studies to the School of Archaeology and Anthropology so as to remove the "dead weight" philological practices presented for "students of post-Chaucerian English literature."[13] Rather, I can see Nietzsche take sides with the lexicographer Henry Cecil Wyld who was convinced that "philology was not a dull subject unless taught in a dull way by dull people," or with Tolkien, who held that even a "bespectacled philologist," "fed on Lautverschiebung and sour Umlaut" would not necessarily lose his "literary soul."[14] Counting on the support of "artists and artistically-minded persons," Nietzsche believes that the

11. "Homer," 3.

12. *On the Art of Writing. Lectures Delivered at the University of Cambridge 1913–14* (Cambridge: Cambridge University Press, 1916), 22.

13. Chadwick is quoted by Chris Baldick, *The Social Mission of English Criticism, 1848–1932* (Oxford: Oxford University Press, 1983), 80.

14. Wyld (1870–1945), the eminent lexicographer, is another voice cited by the *Newbolt Report*, 22. Tolkien's statement is from "Philology," 37.

"magic potion" of historicism, ethics, and aesthetics, which contains an "artistic [. . .] imperative," would not cease to be remixed in order to adapt to new historico-political moments, as it had ever since the founding of the archives in the famed library of Alexandria.[15] Nietzsche would change his mind later, when he fought vicious battles with some of philology's more narrowly scientific representatives, who chastised him for the idiosyncratic mytho-philological "potion" he concocted in *The Birth of Tragedy out of the Spirit of Music* (1872). After 1872 he still appreciated the critical potential of comparative philology which had disempowered the Bible by revealing it as mere man-made literature similar to other ancient literatures: "As a matter of fact," he writes in section 47 of the *Antichrist*, "no man can be a *philologian* or a physician without being also Antichrist. That is to say, as a philologian a man sees *behind* the 'holy books,' and as a physician he sees *behind* the physiological degeneration of the typical Christian. The physician says 'incurable'; the philologian says 'fraud.'"[16] However, while capable of deconstructing the past from a safe distance, he saw philology as inherently incapable of constructing a new future. To renew the mythopoeic language comparative philologists had revealed as merely poetic and past, Nietzsche resigned his position as Professor of Classical Philology and concomitantly abandoned his belief in philology as a method for changing the world. Tellingly, Tolkien and C.S. Lewis would also devote at least part of their activities away from philology and toward mythopoeia. The playful manner in which they did so should not detract from the serious psychological outlet their literary work provided them.

Does philology still serve? Is it more than a remnant of the glory days of the second half of the nineteenth century, although even then, according to Nietzsche, philology may never have presided over more than a "sham monarchy?" Is the term *philology* only residual in the titles of journals, organizations, and institutes that hail from the founding days of various academic humanities disciplines or the Library of Congress

---

15. "Homer," pages 2–3. For a successful history of philological inquiry from the days of the library of Alexandria through the late twentieth century, see Heinz Schlaffer: *Poesie und Wissen. Die Entstehung des ästhetischen Bewußtseins und der philologischen Erkenntnis* (Frankfurt: Suhrkamp, 1990). For survey of philology in the academy, see Hans Ulrich Gumbrecht, *The Powers of Philology. Dynamics of Textual Scholarship* (Urbana: University of Illinois Press, 2003).

16. F. W. Nietzsche, *The Antichrist*, ed. and trans. H. L. Mencken (New York: Knopf, 1920), 136.

catalogue system that classifies everything from "PA" (Classical languages and literatures) through "PZ" (Fiction in English)?[17] Could it be that philology's valuable lessons have been trickling down into the general mindset of *Wikipedia*, the *Online Etymological Dictionary*, or the *European Historical Thesaurus* (*EuroHIT*) in ways that would redefine the term "foundational?" My answer is a resounding "yes," especially when I watch the author of *Éloge de la Variante*, Bernard Cerquiglini, on the world-wide Francophone channel TV 5 Monde explain "chaque jour une curiosité verbale: que la lumière soit faite sur l'origine opaque des mots et expressions de la langue de Racine! Quant aux accords pièges et aux orthographes étranges, le Professeur leur trouve une excuse et nous réconcilie avec le verbe et la règle de grammaire, à coups d'histoires souvent croustillantes."[18] Perhaps even more tellingly, because the ironic use of philological detail presupposes widespread knowledge about words, etyma, and semata, the highly successful North American *Colbert Report*, which features a regular section entitled "The Wørd," would indicate the broad acculturation of philological information. When Stephen Colbert spells *Wørd* with a "slashed 'o,'" discusses elitist vowels, Napoleon Blown Apart, Define and Conquer, Prece-don't, Ideal or No Deal, You-Genics, and Symbol-Minded, he counts on our informed comprehension of the *Joy of Lex* he tries to spread.[19] In fact, his practice follows the spirit of Jacob Grimm, who preferred to study *Sachphilologie* (i.e., studying words in order to learn about entire subjects) to Karl Lachmann's *Wortphilologie* (i.e., studying entire subjects to learn about individual words).[20]

Let me end on one more comparison: During the final scenes of Jean-Jacques Annaud's 1976 Oscar winning comedy, *La victoire en chantant*, two main protagonists, one French and one German, sit together in

---

17. On this issue, see Jonathan Culler, "Anti-Foundational Philology," in *On Philology*, ed. Jan Ziolkowski (University Park: Penn State University Press, 1990), 49–52.

18. Website for the TV 5 Monde television series, *Merci Professeur*, http://www.tv5.org/TV5Site/lf/ merci_professeur.php?id=2583, during which Cerquiglini informs viewers on the history of expressions and individual words in a lively and humorous manner. Accessed on October 21, 2011.

19. I am making reference here to Gyles Brandreth's bestselling book, *The Joy of Lex* (London: Robson, 1987). The various examples of Stephen Colbert's "philological" endeavors are accessible at his Comedy Central website, http://www.colbertnation.com/. Accessed on October 21, 2011.

20. "Rede auf Karl Lachmann," in Jacob Grimm, *Kleinere Schriften*, vol. 1: *Reden und Abhandlungen* (Berlin: F. Dümmler, 1864), 145–62, here 150.

companionable conversation. They have just ceased being at the helm of hostilities between two forgotten and formerly peaceful colonial outposts in West Central Africa. At war for no other reason than that their parent countries had engaged in World War I thousands of miles away, they reflect back on their roles during recent events. Before falling silent in mutual appreciation of their respective roles as nationalistic leaders against their own professional convictions, Hubert Fresnoy, a young geographer from the École Normal Supérieure, confesses to his German counterpart that he is really a socialist and thus a pacifist at heart. In turn, the German Hauptmann Kraft admits to being a disinterested philologist by training. The typological truth of this scene is striking since both characters represent political and academic practices that are today officially extinct in the United States, but whose premises have trickled down into the fabric of the country so that they well up as delightfully inhuman, soulless, and eternally frightening scapegoats, *Them*, for too much government, taxes, and ObamaCare on the one hand and for the isolation of medieval studies from its more theoretically inclined (hence: "hip") colleagues in postmedieval studies on the other.[21] My conclusion is that the philologists may have failed at interpreting the world, eternally disinterested and doggedly busy with "slog," to use Tom Shippey's fitting term[22]; but just like the socialists, they have certainly changed it. The continued dedicated discontent with both their positions leaves no doubt.

---

21. A new journal, *postmedieval*, published by Palgrave Publishers since 2010, aims directly at bridging the chasm between the philological and the postmodern study of the Middle Ages. The 1990s movement of the "New Medievalism" (or "New Philology") had similar, but less far-reaching and interdisciplinary goals.

22. Tom Shippey, *The Road to Middle Earth* (Boston: Houghton Mifflin, 1983), 9.

Really Ancient Druids in British Medievalist Drama

Clare A. Simmons, The Ohio State University

According to her introductory note the setting of Joanna Baillie's two-part drama *Ethwald*, first published in 1802, is "Britain, in the kingdom of Mercia, and the time towards the end of the Heptarchy."[1] Ethwald helps Oswal, King of Mercia, defeat the invading Britons and rises to a position of power in the kingdom. Yet he is still consumed by "One ever-present thought," the prophetic words, "Thou shall be great" (2:181). He asks, "What deep endued seer will draw this veil/ Of dark futurity?" His servant-boy tells him how to find "the female high arch Druid" (2:183), and he enters a cavern filled with "Mystics and Mystic Sisters" to hear the chief Druidess foretell his future greatness.

In the "Address to the Reader" that prefaces the second series of her *Plays of the Passions*, Joanna Baillie, who according to Harriet Martineau some of her contemporaries believed to be "second only to Shakespeare,"[2] explains that since her focus is on universal human emotions, "a time about which comparatively little is well-known" suits her purpose: "I have, therefore, thought, that I might here, without offence, fix my story; here give it a 'habitation and a name,' and model it to my own fancy" (2:x). She then adds, "although I have not adhered to history, the incidents and events of the play will be found, I hope, consistent with the character of the times" (2:x). That may be the case, but a number of historical problems present themselves here. No kings of Mercia were named Oswal or Ethwald, although Penda, named in the drama as a king in the distant

---

1. Joanna Baillie, *A Series of Plays: In which it is attempted to delineate the Stronger Passions of the Mind*, New Edition, 3 vols. (London: Longman, 1821), 2:x. Subsequent references cite this edition by volume and page-number.

2. Harriet Martineau, *Autobiography* (1877), Ed. Linda Peterson (Peterborough, ON: Broadview Press, 2007), 273. Sir Walter Scott was among Baillie's most ardent admirers.

past, died in 655. The invading forces are Britons, not Danes. But even if the play is supposed to take place around the year 750, well before the end of the Heptarchy, how could Druids, who lived in Roman times, still be in existence in Christian Saxon England? This prompts even more questions. Were there ever really Druids, and if so, were any of them Druidesses? And if medievalism is predicated on an opposition between classical and medieval times, how can we account for the presence of Druids in medievalist drama? A brief survey of the representation of dramatic Druids suggests that they become the embodiment, or in some instances the spirit, of national memory, especially memory of the imaginative kind upon which medievalism depends. Medievalism can draw selectively on accepted historical fact and on mythic pasts that sometimes confirm and sometimes contradict historical knowledge; in the case of the Druids, the lines between history and myth are so blurred that Druids become symbolic figures that transcend accepted historical boundaries.

Baillie's Druidess performs this kind of symbolic function as a figure that straddles different aspects of the national past, but at the same time, the play has to account for her physical presence. One way for a Druid, or indeed a female high Arch-Druid, to be around during the medieval period would be for her to be really, really, old, and this particular female high Arch-Druid happens to be "[o]ld, they say, some hundred years or more" (2:184). In this, surprising as it may seem at first, she is far from alone. In British and Irish drama of the later eighteenth and early nineteenth century, Druids defy chronology, the usual lifespan of humanity, and standard ideas about religion; they become, in fact, a locus for what Katie Trumpener has called "Bardic Nationalism," the link between the poetic, the primitive, and national memory.[3] This essay briefly considers eighteenth-century and Romantic-era British ideas about Druids and the ways in which these preservers of national wisdom become a means of talking about both the continuities and disjunctions so central to medievalism.

Who were the Druids? As Stuart Piggott and Ronald Hutton have remarked, we have no archaeological evidence that they ever existed,

---

3. Katie Trumpener, *Bardic Nationalism: The Romantic Novel and the British Empire*. (Princeton: Princeton University Press, 1997). Trumpener's main focus is on how the poetic culture of Britain's "Celtic peripheries" affects the history the novel, enabling the dominant culture to be defined by its margins: she notes that for "nationalist antiquaries, the bard is the mouthpiece of the whole society," 6.

although accounts in classical sources, particularly Caesar and Tacitus, suggest that they probably did, and that in ancient Celtic society, priestly diviners and lawgivers played an important role.[4] A. L. Owen points out in his comprehensive study of literary interpretations of the Druids that English antiquaries had only two classical sources specifically discussing British Druids, the accounts of Julius Caesar and Tacitus.[5] The most frequently mentioned "facts" about the Druids are drawn from Caesar's *Gallic War* and apply to both British and continental European Druids, Caesar explaining that the "discipline" of Druidry developed in Britain and spread to the rest of Gaul. According to Caesar, the Druids were the priests and lawgivers of their people; they were exempt from military service; they worshipped in groves; they believed in the transmigration of souls. Finally, Caesar explains that Druids supervise the Gauls' human sacrifices, sometimes by enclosing people in giant figures of men made out of twigs. Caesar thus portrays the society of the Gauls as having organized structures, but as below the Romans in terms of civilization.[6]

For British readers in the eighteenth and nineteenth centuries, the question was whether the Druids represented a continuity of British identity or whether they marked a disjuncture between Celtic Britain and Saxon and Norse times. In the most-read British history of the eighteenth century, Hume's *History of England*, David Hume does not have much to say about the Druids, except to show how much he dislikes them. Hume imagines a people entirely bound by mysterious laws: "They practised their rites in dark groves, or other secret recesses; and, in order to throw a greater mystery over their religion, they communicated their doctrines only to the initiated, and strictly forbad the committing of them to writing, lest they should at any time be exposed to the examination of the profane

---

4. For an overview of historical and mythical ideas about the Druids, see Stuart Piggott, *The Druids* (1968; New York: Thames and Hudson, 1975) and Ronald Hutton's *Blood and Mistletoe: The History of the Druids in Britain* (New Haven: Yale University Press, 2009). Both point out that although archaeological evidence supports the idea of priest-led ritual among the Celtic peoples contemporary with the Romans, archaeology has yet to find evidence even labeling these priests as Druids, or to support the Roman contention that Druidry was an organized structure among the Gauls.

5. A. L. Owen, *The Famous Druids: A Survey of Three Centuries of English Literature on the Druids* (Oxford: Clarendon, 1962), 15.

6. C. Julius Caesar, *Gallic War*. With a translation by H. J. Edwards (London: Heinemann, c.1917), 6:13–16.

vulgar."[7] The Druids thus control law by keeping it as mystery. Their determination to be "pre-historic" by not writing down their secrets had earlier infuriated John Milton, who, probably drawing on Caesar's reference to their use of Greek letters for non-religious purposes believed that the Druids knew Greek and therefore could see no reason why they did not write things down.[8] Finally, Druids show their lack of humane feeling by practicing human sacrifice. Hume is paraphrasing Caesar throughout this passage; he cannot, however, refrain from adding a sentence not in his source. "Thus," Hume sarcastically concludes, "the bands of government, which were naturally loose among that rude and turbulent people, were happily corroborated by the terrors of their superstition" (Hume, 1:5). For Hume, the Druids demonstrate combined spiritual and legal authority at its worst, using superstition to control impulses towards liberty.

About the same time, Edmund Burke began an "Abridgement of English History," which is even more hostile in its reading of the Druids, but does give a possible origin for ideas about female Druids. One of the few records of specifically British Druids is Tacitus' account of Paulinus' slaughter of the Druids on the island of Mona:

> Stabat pro litore diversa acies, densa armis virisque, intercursantibus feminis; in modum Furiarum veste ferali, crinis deiectis faces praeferebant; Druidaeque circum, preces diras sublatis ad caelum manibus fundentes, novitate aspectus perculere militum, ut quaesi haerentibus membris immobile corpus vulneribus praeberent.[9]

A fairly literal translation might read:

> A diverse battleline stood on the shore, a thick mass of weapons and men, with women running in and out; in the manner of Furies, with their savage costumes and dishevelled hair, they brandished torches; and the Druids standing round them,[10] pouring out dire prayers with their hands raised to heaven, presented such a strange

---

7. David Hume, *The History of England*, 12 vols. (London: Washbourne, 1844), 1:3.

8. John Milton, *History of Britain: that part especially now call'd England, from the traditional beginning, continu'd to the Norman Conquest* (1677; London: Wilks, 1818), 2–3. Caesar had suggested that the Druids knew Greek letters.

9. Cornelius Tacitus, *Annales* pages 13–16. With a translation by John Jackson (London: Heinemann, 1937), 14:30.

10. I am reading *circum* as "round them," although some interpreters have read this as "about" and others as "in a circle." The latter was most attractive to the eighteenth-century antiquaries who associated Druids with circles.

sight to the soldiers, that as though their limbs were paralyzed, motionless, they exposed their bodies to wounds. (*Annals* 14:30)

In Burke's rendering, this becomes:

> On every side of the British army were seen bands of Druids in their most sacred habits surrounding the troops, lifting their hands to heaven, devoting to death their enemies, and animating their disciples to religious frenzy by the uncouth ceremonies of a savage ritual, and the horrid mysteries of a superstition familiar with blood. The female Druids also moved about, in a troubled order, their hair dishevelled, their garments torn, torches in their hands, and, with an horror increased by the perverted softness of their sex, howled out the same curses and imprecations with greater clamour. Astonished at the sight, the Romans for some time neither advanced nor returned the darts of the enemy.[11]

Burke was possibly misled by "Druidae," since first declension words are usually feminine, but the mistranslation is characteristic of Burke's ideas about gender roles. As in the *Reflections on the Revolution in France*, where he laments the treatment of the French queen and concludes that "the age of chivalry is gone,"[12] Burke presents a failure to differentiate between the roles of the sexes as evidence of a lack of civilization. Even though this involves describing female Druids whose presence is distinctly questionable in his source, Burke's translation stresses that the Romans' terror was increased by this female deviance: "the perverted softness of their sex" is pure Burke. Burke's horror at the Druids may also be due to a personal need to root out "Celtic" influences in his model of Britishness: his Druids are pointedly nothing like Britons of his day.

Yet even before Burke composed his historical fragment, a more sympathetic view of the Druids had emerged. Literary works probably owed most to druidic enthusiasts such as William Stukeley, who combined a

---

11. Edmund Burke, *Abridgement of English History*, *Works* (Boston: Little, Brown, 1886), 195–96.

12. Edmund Burke, *Reflections on the Revolution in France*, new edition (London, 1793), 61. Burke here alludes to the lack of respect paid to the queen of France, but he has slightly earlier described the royal captives as being escorted "amidst the horrid yells, and shrilling screams, and frantic dances, and infamous contumelies, and all the unutterable abominations of the furies of hell, in the abused shape of the vilest of women" (57–8). signs that the Revolution has "inverted order in all things" (56). The focus on the supposed female Druids is thus in keeping with Burkes horror at women in the political realm.

talent for archaeological observance with role-playing in which he and his friends were Druids.[13] Stukeley ascribed to the Druids most of the structures of British pre-history, notably standing stones and barrows, but particularly Stonehenge and Avebury.[14] Very possibly because many of the structures that Stukeley mentioned were circular, Druids become associated with circles, and this idea has tended to prevail, even in the Loeb translation of Tacitus, which translates "circum" as "in a circle" when it could just be "round about." In middle life, Stukeley abandoned his earlier occupation of medical doctor and took orders in the Church of England. He published his extensively illustrated *Stonehenge: A Temple Restor'd to the British Druids* in 1740 and *Abury, A Temple of the British Druids, with Some Others Describ'd* in 1743, representing both his archaeological researches and his ideas about British druidic authority that were to influence most later ideas about British druidic practice. Stukeley imagined an entire Druid culture that was solidly British and monotheistic; far from being obscure and bloodthirsty practitioners of human sacrifice, his Druids were good churchmen like himself.[15] Before Stukeley's time, some people had believed that Merlin had built Stonehenge; not everyone was prepared to abandon such a pleasing idea, so that maybe Merlin built Stonehenge for the Druids, or maybe he was a Druid too.[16]

The rehabilitation of the Druids was such that by the late eighteenth century, some enthusiasts formed Neo-Druid groups. Foremost among these was a craftsman named Edward Williams, better known by the bardic name he chose for himself, Iolo Morganwg. Ronald Hutton has noted the centrality of Iolo's role in Neo-Druidism, which he seems

---

13. See Hutton, *Blood and Mistletoe*, 86–102.

14. This is especially frustrating to Stuart Piggott, who repeatedly points out that Stonehenge is much earlier than the Druids. Stukeley was not the first to connect Stonehenge with the Druids; John Aubrey had earlier made a similar connection (Hutton, *Blood and Mistletoe*, 66–8, 89).

15. William Stukeley, *Stonehenge: A Temple Restor'd to the British Druids* (1740); *Abury, A Temple of the British Druids, with Some Others Describ'd* (1743). See also Stuart Piggott, *William Stukeley, An Eighteenth-Century Antiquarian*, Revised edition (London: Thames and Hudson, 1970).

16. For example, John Wood's *Choir Gaure, Vulgarly Called Stonehenge, on Salisbury Plain, Described, Restored, and Explained* (London, 1747) attributes Stonehenge to the Druids. Although he rejects the idea found in Geoffrey of Monmouth's writings that Merlin built Stonehenge, in using phrases such as "Merlin, probably the then Arch-Prophet of Britain" (118), he does not seem entirely to have dismissed Merlin's historical existence.

largely to have invented,[17] including the three orders of Druids, Bards, and Ovates.[18] Whereas Stukeley envisioned the Druids as a priestly class who were true forerunners of the Church of England, Iolo saw druidism as a popular form of democratic resistance to hierarchy and central to his own Welsh heritage. Iolo produced translations of the supposedly ancient writings of Taliesin, which in the Ossianic tradition seem to have been inspired by some genuine medieval sources but were probably largely his own composition. In the 1790s Iolo helped form a group of Druids who "worshipped the sun" and recited druidic poetry on Primrose Hill, the highest geographic point in London.[19] The poet and visionary William Blake was acquainted with these Druids and also, I believe, with Stukeley's ideas,[20] which influence many of his writings.

Naturally playwrights started to realize that Druids had audience appeal. Some playwrights came up with historical subjects where Druids would not be too far beyond the possibility of chronology. For example, William Mason's *Caractacus* (1759) tells how when driven from his kingdom the British king takes refuge with the druids of Mona, and plans to become a Druid himself, telling the chief Druid that he would rather be a Druid, or even a sacred oak, than a king:

> Druid, these groves
> Have caught the dismal colouring of my soul,
> Changing their dark dun garbs to very sable,
> In pity to their guest. Hail, hallow'd oaks!
> Hail, British born! Who, last of British race,
> Hold your primaeval rights by nature's charter;
> Not at the nod of Caesar.[21]

---

17. Iolo Morganwg, *Iolo Manuscripts, A Selection of the Ancient Welsh Manuscripts, In Prose and Verse, from the collection made by the late Edward Williams, Iolo Morganwyg.* Ed. Taliesin Williams. (Llandovry: Reeb, 1848). See also Hutton, *Blood and Mistletoe*, 150–72.

18. The terms derive from Caesar, but Iolo seems to have invented their responsibilities and clothing. A mark of the growing prevalence of the Orders is that they are not mentioned in F. Sayers's 1790 *Dramatic Sketches*, but are explained in the 1803 edition.

19. See Deena Taylor, "A Note on William Blake and the Druids of Primrose Hill," *Blake: An Illustrated Quarterly*. (Winter 1983–84), 104–5.

20. See my discussion of Blake's use of Stukeley's topological ideas in *Popular Medievalism in Romantic-Era Britain* (New York: Palgrave Macmillan, 2011), 38–42.

21. William Mason, *Caractacus, A Dramatic Poem* (London, 1759), 31.

Other plays, such as the American James M'Henry's *The Usurper, An Historical Tragedy* (1829) and James Cartwright Cross's *The Round Tower; or, The Chieftains of Ireland* (1809), both retell the story of the Irish king Cartha or Cobthach. According to much later medieval stories, Cobthach received bad advice from, in M'Henry's words, an "unprincipled druid, whom he raised from the lowest station in life"[22] and who advised him to murder his brother and usurp the throne. In M'Henry's play, the Arch-Druid is a thorough villain who states that "Both reason and experience have convinced me/ That guilt and punishment have no existence,/But in men's fancies" (2:1). The play seems reluctant, though, to dismiss all Druids as villains; the Arch-Druid is a hypocrite, but the story also features a sincere Priestess, who takes virtue and religion seriously.

According to the chronicles the story of Cobthach takes place in the third century before the common era, the time actually associated with the Celtic religion that could be called druidic. Cross's pantomime[23] *The Round Tower*, however, moves the story into the Middle Ages: Cobthach and the Druids are coexistent with some Viking-like Danes, and the scenery includes ruins, graveyards, and a round tower with a drawbridge. Cobthach's treachery has already taken place when the drama begins; in the end, both the usurper and Danes are defeated, the rightful ruler restored, and "Druids and Priests" form "a picturesque group" to sing, "Long may virtue reign,/Love ever bless the plain,/Huzza! Our king for ever" (scene 17).

Cross's *Round Tower* preserves the existence of Druids by locating them in an indistinct Middle Ages, and such was the draw of Druids that a surprising number of authors wanted to imagine them surviving into the post-Roman period. In the 1790s F. Sayers wrote a trilogy of dramatic poems that demonstrate his interest in Norse mythology, published as *Dramatic Sketches of Northern Mythology*; the work is heavily indebted to Thomas Percy's *Northern Antiquities*, which had appeared in 1765. Sayers was a friend of Robert Southey and William Taylor, and at this time, they were all intrigued by the Gothic tradition; Southey's voluminous poetical

---

22. James M'Henry, *The Usurper, An Historical Tragedy in Five Acts* (Philadelphia: J. Haraday, 1829), Preface. Subsequent references follow this edition.

23. James Cartwright Cross, *The Round Tower* (London: Printed for Author, 1809). The play is described as a "pantomime ballet," with seventeen scenes of Romantic landscape and a number of songs. Druids frequently form part of the setting, and the chief Druid sings a song.

works were to include a selection of ballads, while Taylor was to become known as the translator of Bürger's "Lenore." In the physician Frank Sayers's case, after wrestling with reconciling his strictly Classical training with Northern mythology, as it was then termed, he turned away from it to become a convinced Classicist, ending his life as an ardent and orthodox Anglican.[24] Sayers's experiments in recreating bardic song in the Norse tradition merit more attention from medievalists than they have hitherto received; my main concern here, though, is on his references to the Druids. The first drama in the trilogy, *The Descent of Freya*, is, as its title suggests, purely Norse in its subject-matter. In the second, *Moina*, however, Sayers decided to combine his Northern mythologies. The title-character Moina is a Celtic woman who has been kidnapped and forcibly married to a cruel Saxon called Harold, of whom she remarks, "To slay, to conquer, these are Harold's pleasures,/ To stain his dark-blue steel in human gore."[25] Harold has the support of a chorus of bardic priests who chant hymns to Odin and the other Norse gods while preserving the classical Greek dramatic unities; hence unlike Mason's *Caractacus*, where Druids and Bards form a continuum, in this play they represent two different religions. Although no druids appear as characters in the drama, Moina speaks fondly of the sacred woods and of the Druids as the priests of her native land (32). She characterizes her native religion as one of peaceful groves and the Saxon religion as one of slaughter and feasting, but nevertheless, she herself threatens violence when she says:

> Thou unseen power, who in my country's woods
> In ancient silence dwell'st, whom trembling druids
> With hallow'd rites invoke, arise, arise,
> And wing with hissing dart to Harold's bosom—(36).
> Although Moina believes that Harold killed her lover Carrill in battle, in fact Carrill was restored to health by friendly Druids and, disguised as a Bard, he comes to rescue her (49). When Carrill

---

24. On Sayers's relationship with the Gothic, see Douglass H. Thomson's "A Note on One of the Earliest Gothic Ballads: Frank Sayers's 'Sir Egwin,'" *Papers on Language and Literature* 46:2 (2010), 195–229. A. Dwight Culler quotes William Taylor as crediting Sayers as the first to write "monodramas" in English, but are modeled after Greek tragedy. See A. Dwight Culler, "Monodrama and the Dramatic Monologue," *PMLA* 90 (1975), 376–77.

25. F. [Frank] Sayers, *Dramatic Sketches of Northern Mythology* (London, 1790). Quotations follow the 3rd edition, *Poems, Containing Sketches of Northern Mythology, Etc.* (Norwich: Stevenson and Matchett, 1803), 32.

first makes himself known to Moina, she insists that since she is now married to Harold, she must remain his wife:

'tho force compell'd me
To share the bed of Harold, whilst he breathes
I'm his alone, nor shall my sacred honour
Be ever blasted. (53)

Once Moina learns that Harold has died in battle, however, she expresses the hope that a "white-robed druid" will marry her to Carrill (59). At the same time, Carrill consults a "prophetess" who tells him of Harold's death and foretells that this day "Moina's woes shall be at peace" (63). Although this aged prophetess identifies herself as a follower of Harold and not a Druidess, her prophecy has a similar ambiguity to what Baillie's character foretells. The Bards uphold Saxon law by burying Moina alive with Harold, and Carrill, announcing, "Carrill hastes to join/ Thy gloomy ghost," jumps off a cliff (79).[26]

Druids finally appear onstage in Sayers's third play, *Starno*. His Preface explains:

The story of the following Tragedy, like that of [*Moina*}, is fictitious, but I hope not entirely inconsistent with the manners and customs of the Celtic people. As the scene of action is laid in Britain, I have been obliged to desert the mythology of the Saxons for the institutions and ceremonies of the druids; some of these ceremonies have already been received by the public with delight, as displayed in the admirable tragedy of [Mason's] Caractacus; but although the variety and magnificence of the Gothic religion is by no means rivaled by the Celtic, yet there appeared to me some parts of it untouched, which might be introduced into dramatic poetry with tolerable effect. (101-2)

Sayers's preference for the Norse religion over druidism is evident in what follows, even though by the third edition the drama begins with a huge introductory footnote suggesting that Druidic practices might have common ancestry with Brahminism and that the Celts "were originally an oriental people" (110). The notes suggest the common origins of religion, and indeed, the Druid priests in *Starno* call their god Hesus, provocatively close to Jesus. The Briton Starno, a Celtic name that Sayers might have found in James Macpherson's 1765 "Ossian" poems, decides

---

26. In following the example of the self-destruction of Gray's Bard, Carrill ironically assumes the bardic identity he has previously imitated.

to give the Druids a captive for human sacrifice. As the Druids explain, "The fearless soul of Starno/Shall glut its vengeance in the gushing blood of foes" (111). Unfortunately, the person he selects is his daughter Dauna's Saxon lover Kelric. When Starno, affected by his daughter's grief, changes his mind, the Druid chorus inform him:

> If thou fear'st not heaven, yet dread our power;
> Soon shall our lips pronounce the just decree
> Thy crime deserves. —Never by the altar more
> Thy foot accurs'd shall stand; no more thy clan
> Shall know their chief . . . (131)

Rather than make Starno an outcast from his people and from religion, Kelric says that he is willing to die; Daura commits suicide off-stage, and Kelric urges the Druid-priest to kill him. As he dies, Kelric envisions both lovers wandering "in Valhalla's groves," combining the divine places of the Druid and Saxon religions.

Sayers does not directly mention the age of his Druids. Julius Caesar explicitly states that young men sign up eagerly to train to be Druids, although the process of instruction can be as long as twenty years.[27] If no Druids were actually young, some according to this account would have been middle aged. In medievalist drama, though, Druids are emphatically old. One such example is the work of James Mylne, a Scottish tenant-farmer who was marketed as a "natural" poet and who seems to have had aspirations of being a second Robert Burns. Mylne's play *The British Kings, A Tragedy* was never performed, as far as I have been able to determine, and shows a distinctly eccentric vision of the early medieval past. The play centers on the conflict between Cadwallan, King of the Britons, and Osricke, the adopted son of King of Northumberland. According to the chronicles, Cadwallan died in the 630s, some forty years after the arrival of Augustine of Canterbury yet after the time traditionally ascribed to King Arthur, so no consistency should be looked for in the chronology. Cadwallan encounters a Druid who has been in his cave for "four score winters" and has "twice told . . . the natural age of man."[28] The 140-year-old Druid, who hardly surprisingly is "the last of his race," discloses to Cadwallan that Osricke is actually the British king's long-lost

---

27. Caesar, 6:14.

28. James Mylne, *Poems, Consisting of Miscellaneous Pieces, and Two Tragedies* (Edinburgh, 1790), 147.

son; Cadwallan, who has raped Osricke's love, Lena, allows Osricke to kill him, and Osricke and Lena also die. Fortunately, Prince Arthur appears in the fifth Act and takes the throne to unify Britain. The ancient Druid, who also dispenses herbs to alleviate Lena's madness, has the last words of the play:

> Your children's children, and their latest race
> Shall bless you the first founders of this union,
> For, when the island all shall so unite,
> Old seers fortel, that Britain's power shall stride
> From the sun's rising to his setting place. (238)

Yet Mylnes's 140-year-old Druid is a young sprig compared with the band of Druids in William Sotheby's *The Cambrian Hero, or Llewelyn the Great* (1800), which takes place in the reign of Edward I. Prince Llewelyn, in retreat from the English, determines to consult an "old Sybil" who is "versed it is said in Merlin's prescient lore" and learn Wales's future. When he finds the Sybil, she says, "I knew thou'dst come" and explains,

> Those holy druids—high heaven's first-born priests—
> They—who are waiting in king Arthur's court—
> And for a thousand years have been confined
> In a dark cave—I'the bowels of the earth—
> Them did I call—and now thy fate is fixed. . .[29]

The stage directions read, "Sybil forms a circle in the air with her wand. Four Druids start out of the cave, attired in white vestments: they range on each side of the soothsayer, and sing, with appropriate music, the following stanzas; Llewelyn, at the same time, regarding them with amazement"—amazement being a likely emotion at the sight of thousand-year-old Druids. Notably here, though, Druids are placed alongside Arthurian legend, and the Sybil herself is associated both with druidic prognostication and with Merlin. As usual, the Sybil's prophecy ("Thou shalt through London's streets triumphant ride") is ambiguous, and the Druid's advice in their song, which urges Llewelyn to "rouse, and strike the blow," unhelpful, since the "Cambrian Hero" is defeated. Yet even though Druids seemed to be good box office, Drury Lane had not had much financial success with Sotheby's work and passed on this play entirely.[30]

29. William Sotheby, *The Cambrian Hero, or, Llewelyn the Great* (Egham, 1800), 68.
30. See Sidney Lee and Melanie Ord, "William Sotheby," *Oxford Dictionary of National*

Druids did, however, appear onstage in the masque *The Institution of the Order of the Garter*. The Genius of Britain tells an assembled group of Bards and Spirits that it:

> Must here await th'approach of other Spirits,
> Sage Druids, Britain's old philosophers,
> Who still enamour'd of their ancient haunts
> Unseen of mortal eyes, they hover round
> Their ruin'd altars, and these sacred oaks...[31]

The altars and oaks apparently did not exclude Druids from the Christian heaven, which implies that the author, like Stukeley, accepted that their religion was based on some kind of divine revelation. The Chief Druid who appears explains that "Our country's weal, ev'n from the bliss of heaven,/Can charm down patriot souls to visit earth" (4), which accounts for why Druids can appear in the reign of Edward I (these Druids bear Edward no animosity for England's annexation of Wales). The Druids and Bards are present as Edward sees a vision of Britain's future. This includes the institution of the Order of the Garter, which Edward I presents to his son; the spirits of Bards and Druids having returned to heaven, the masque ends with references to actual medieval texts describing the institution of the order of the Garter.

The references to Edward I in these last two plays suggest that playwrights did not distinguish too carefully between Bards and Druids, and when they did, as in the case of Sayers's *Moina* and Iolo's three categories, the distinctions were invented. As the language of Sotheby's *Cambrian Hero* suggests, Thomas Gray's 1757 poem "The Bard" is an influence on later depictions of both Bards and Druids. "The Bard" is mainly in the voice of the last of the Welsh bards, who according to what Gray calls "a tradition current in Wales," Edward I had ordered killed to secure his conquest of Wales.[32] In the early 1800s, even though most of them were aware that this story was not literally true,[33] poets clung to it as a repre-

---

Biography Online, www.oxforddnb.com.proxy.lib.ohio-state.edu/view/article/26038 (accessed May 8, 2011).

31. Gilbert West, *The Institution of the Order of the Garter* (London, 1742); David Garrick later produced a version of the masque.

32. Thomas Gray, "The Bard," *Poetical Works*, 2nd edition (London: Whittingham, 1800), 32–48.

33. For example, Felicia Hemans's poem "Chant of the Bards before their Massacre by Edward I," written in the 1820s, adds a footnote, "This sanguinary deed is not attested

sentation of the power of poetry to preserve the spirit of a nation. The figure of the Bard, who in Gray's poem leaps from Snowdon into "endless night," hence marks the attempted erasure of the historical past and its survival in imagination. Because their existence in the Middle Ages implies longevity both of the body and of national and cultural memory, Druids become the ultimate embodiment of this bardic tradition, and drama seeks a variety of ingenious and ingenuous ways to bring them into the medieval world. As Ronald Hutton has shown, the seemingly eccentric idea of medieval Druids has survived into the contemporary world in the form of environmentally-active groups, such as the Secular Order of Druids (acronym SOD), whose beliefs integrate druids, King Arthur, Stonehenge, and a love of nature.[34] In "Medievalisms and Why They Matter," Tom Shippey writes that there are "many medievalisms in the world, and some of them are as safe as William Morris wallpaper: but not all of them."[35] Druids mark the dangerous confrontation of the past. Like Gray's Bard, Druids stand on the edge, between ancient and medieval times, between England and its Celtic fringe, between superstition and religion, between past, present, and future, and between loss and survival. Druids may not be medieval, but they are medievalism.

---

by any historian of credit." Felicia Hemans, *Poetical Works* (London: Nimmo, 1875), 151.

34. Neo-Druids of the present day often practice civil disobedience, claiming that their freedom of worship and access to traditionally common land (notably at sites such as Stonehenge) is restricted; they also participate in environmental issues. They are thus claiming to respond to a different law, namely that of the Nature-Goddess, and as Ronald Hutton has pointed out, at least one of these groups, led by Arthur Uther Pendragon, sees medievalism and Druidry as one and the same, a recreation (or rebirth) of earlier British experience. Hutton tells how Arthur changed his name when an experience at Stonehenge convinced him that he was the King's reincarnation: "He then asked The Goddess to help him recover Excalibur by the next full moon, accepting that if he did he would commit himself to the defense of the land. On the day before the moon reached its fullness, he saw a sword offered for sale in a shop window, which had been made to represent Excalibur in a film. He bought it, and vowed from that moment to fight for civil liberties and environmental issues." Ronald Hutton, "The New Druids," *The Year's Work in Medievalism 1999*, 16–18.

35. Tom Shippey, "Medievalisms and Why they Matter," *Studies in Medievalism* 17 (2009), 52. A version of this essay was presented in a panel honoring Tom Shippey's wise, generous, and learned contribution to the study of Medievalism at the Medieval Convention at the University of Western Michigan, 2010.

Neomedievalisms in Tom Phillips' *Commedia* Illustrations

Karl Fugelso

ON OTHER OCCASIONS, I have defined neomedievalism as responses to responses to the Middle Ages.[1] In the course of giving examples and refining that definition, I have mentioned Tom Phillips' interpretation of William Blake's third of three illustrations for *Inferno* 22.[2] In this paper I would like to expand on that example and to look at the many other variations on neomedievalism in Phillips' 138 images of Dante's text. I thereby hope to strengthen my definition even as I raise questions about its range and applicability.

Phillips began his illustrations in 1976 to "guide forward a steady reading" of his accompanying translation of the *Inferno* and to "enhance its pleasure by pointing the reader to unexpected connections, both of mood and meaning," as he says in the introduction to his notes for the 1985 edition of his 1983 livre d'artiste.[3] The images range in method and

   1. I made this suggestion at the 22nd Annual International Conference on Medievalism in London, Ontario, and in the version of that presentation for *The Year's Work in Medievalism* 22 (2008), 55–61.

   2. For widely available reproductions of Blake's *Commedia* illustrations, which he produced from approximately 1824 to his death in 1826, see The *Divine Comedy*: William Blake, ed. David Bindman (Paris: Bibliothèque de l'Image, 2000); or the unedited William Blake's *Divine Comedy* Illustrations (Mineola, NY: Dover, 2008). For widely available reproductions of Phillips' *Commedia* images, see the reference below to the Thames and Hudson edition of his livre d'artiste.

   3. Phillips' livre d'artiste, which was issued by his own Talfourd Press in 1983 for 10,000 pounds sterling, was reissued by Thames and Hudson (New York) in 1985 for a far smaller price and with new notes by Phillips, albeit with smaller images. All of my parenthetical page references to his remarks come from the later edition, including its "Introduction to the notes," which is essentially the prospectus announcing the earlier edition.

material from graphite drawing and watercolor painting to newspaper collage and silkscreen transfers, but they are consistent in the sophistication with which they refract Dante's text through contemporary and historical contexts. Indeed, as Phillips attempts to provide what he terms "a bridge in time and reference" (283), he invokes an extraordinarily wide array of artists and writers. He constructs a veritable primer on how at least one aspect of the Middle Ages, the *Commedia*, influenced numerous post-medieval intellectuals.

Perhaps the most evident, least complex examples of his neomedievalism are his references to medievalizing texts and/or authors. And within that category, perhaps the clearest instance of neomedievalism is to be found in his second of four illustrations for *Inferno* 27. Across from his translation of Dante's introduction to the fraudulent counselor Guido da Montefeltro, and beneath a frame formed by a "river of eloquence" that "start[s] in the top left hand corner in its original colour and progressively twist[s] itself into a cunning tongue of flame" (303), Phillips has quoted a fragment of T. S. Eliot's "Love Song of J. Alfred Prufrock." Eliot's epigram for that poem is taken from this canto where Guido says, "If I believed my answer was addressed to one who might go back into the world this flame would stop vibrating and stand still," and Phillips claims that in referencing "Prufrock" he "repays one of Eliot's many compliments to his favourite poet of the past" (303).[4] That is, Phillips quotes a post-medieval text with full awareness that it references the same medieval text on which he himself dwells.

He makes similar claims for his third of four illustrations for *Inferno* 17, but in this case his neomedievalism is complicated by the fact that he parodies, rather than quotes, his post-medieval source. Directly across from his translation of the Pilgrim's encounter with the usurers and with Geryon, Phillips depicts the upper façade of the Scrovegni Chapel, which was erected by the son of one of the three main usurers described by Dante. Above the façade is a blue sky with gold stars like those designed by Giotto for the chapel ceiling, and at the bottom of the illustration are black flames pierced by the stenciled inscription "Oh Ezra remember how came by Usura Cappella Scrovegni & skies of Giotto." The Ezra to whom the inscription refers is of course Ezra Pound, and, as Phillips noted in 1985 (296), the inscription as a whole is a satire as well as refutation of

---

4. This excerpt of Phillips' translation of the *Commedia* appears on page 303 amid his acknowledgment of referencing Eliot.

Pound's reply to Dante that "Not by Usura came [a host of art and craft treasures]."[5] Iconographic neomedievalism merges with stylistic neomedievalism, as content that references medievalist content is couched in such a fashion as to play off the form in which the iconographic medievalism is presented.

Even more complex—and perhaps even more playful—neomedievalism may be found in Phillips' third of four illustrations for *Inferno* 7. Directly across from the discussion by Virgil and Dante of Fortune and avarice, Phillips stenciled what he calls the "semi-gibberish" of Plutus (290), as well as variations on it, in nineteen gray rows against a black background. Surrounding these lines are thirty-six gray balls filled with abstract, branching forms in dark gray-brown, light gray-brown, and off-white. And in the center of lines six through eight is an excerpt from a review in the *Times Literary Supplement*. As Phillips noted in 1985, this excerpt testifies to the fact that James Joyce acknowledged the babble of Dante's Plutus as license for Joyce's own experiments in language (290). And, as Phillips went on to point out in 1985, the stenciled text plays with Plutus' words in the manner of Walter Arensberg, whose famous *Cryptography of Dante* is described by Phillips as "a bewildering farrago of false wordtrails pursued with earnest lunacy" (290). Thus, an artist claims that his content refers to an author, Joyce, who is medievalist in the sense that he allowed the medieval author at the core of the artist's work, Dante, to free him, Joyce, for verbal experimentation. And the artist echoes that freedom via a more direct invocation of the verbal play of another medievalist, Arensberg, who also responds to the medieval text at the heart of the artist's work. Iconographic neomedievalism joins again with stylistic neomedievalism, but this time in the intersection of: 1) content acknowledging the influence of a medieval text on the form and content of a post-medieval author, and 2) the form around that neomedievalist content echoing the medievalist manner in the response by a second (or, if we see Phillips as an author, third) post-medieval author to the same medieval text that inspired the first (or second) post-medieval author.

Yet as complex as is the neomedievalism in those two overlapping references to medievalist texts, it pales in comparison to that in many of Phillips' responses to images of medieval subjects. Even his simplest, clearest allusion to a particular post-medieval depiction of a medieval

---

5. For Pound's remark, see his Canto XLV.

subject may have ambiguities that occlude determination of whether—and, if so, how—that post-medieval image is a response to the Middle Ages. For example, Phillips says he based his image of Pope Boniface VIII in the third of four illustrations for *Inferno* 27 on a drawing he made in the foyer of the Museo Poldi Pezzoli, Milan, "where a poster featured [Boniface's] equestrian statue" (303). The presence of the poster in the Museo would suggest the statue was medieval. And, in fact, the bust and hand extending down toward the lower right from the upper left corner of Phillips' illustration look rather medieval in their blocky outline and lack of detail. But without further knowledge of precisely which poster Phillips copied, or at least which equestrian statue might be designated by his implication that there is only one for Boniface, we cannot be sure that the statue is medieval, the poster is medievalist, and Phillips' references to it are neomedievalist.[6]

Moreover, even if we determine that the statue is, in fact, medieval, Phillips may not be a neomedievalist in responding to the poster, for the latter may not count as medievalism. At least some interpreters may be reluctant to see it as a response to the Middle Ages if it merely refers to the statue through unaltered photographs taken from the most conventional of viewpoints in the most conventional of methods. Though other critics might point out that the very selection of this statue for reproduction, not to mention the choices to follow convention, count as interpretation and therefore medievalism, the issue is at least debatable and allows that, in this case, Phillips may be a medievalist rather than neomedievalist.

Of course, if we view the poster as departing from whatever might count as an objective rendering of the statue, and if the statue is indeed medieval, then there can be no doubt that the poster represents stylistic as well as iconographic medievalism and that Phillips is, in this instance, a two-fold neomedievalist. But the same may not be true for his many references to nineteenth- and twentieth-century illustrations of the *Commedia*, for the fact that the contents of those illustrations do not revolve around a medieval image allows that their style may not fully incorporate medievalism. For example, Phillips quotes from Gustave Doré's mid-nineteenth-century *Commedia* engravings on at least three occasions: in the lower third of his fourth of four illustrations for *Inferno* 6, wherein "the cold compress of [gluttons] beneath the monotonously falling rain, hail

---

6. This is assuming, of course, that the subject of his drawing in the foyer was the poster.

and snow is a collage of fragments of figures taken from a cheap reprint of Doré's version of the *Inferno*" (289); in his fourth of four illustrations for *Inferno* 21, wherein a "self-explanatory confection of collaged fragments of Doré's illustrations" form the background and goose-stepping figure of Barbariccia making a trumpet of his anus (298); and in the background of his fourth of four illustrations for *Inferno* 23, wherein the "hints" of cowled hypocrites behind the supine figure of Caiaphas come from fragments of Doré's illustrations (300).[7] In every one of these cases, Phillips undoubtedly acts as an iconographic neomedievalist, for he incorporates another post-medieval illustrator's *Commedia* subject matter. And Phillips may be a stylistic neomedievalist to the degree that he adapts Doré's subject matter and responds to Doré's non-iconographic efforts to capture the medieval spirit of Dante's text. Indeed, even if Doré had not shaped his presentation towards those ends, Phillips may be a stylistic neomedievalist to the degree that he at least believed Doré did so. But Phillips may not be a neomedievalist in the sense of someone who responds to medievalist means put towards medievalist ends, for though Doré may pursue the medieval effect of Dante's text, he does not necessarily do so by medievalist strategies or medievalist techniques. In fact, Doré very much presented himself as an artist of his own time and was famous for decidedly non-medievalist innovations in style and technique, such as the wash effects created by him and his engravers.[8] Of course, Phillips may still be a neomedievalist in the sense of someone who responds to what he believes are medievalist means put towards medievalist ends, for he may not have been aware that Doré applied avant-garde strategies and techniques towards medievalist ends. But such a blind spot would be extraordinary for an artist with Phillips' comparatively profound knowledge of art history, and it does not, in any case, equate to the sort of stylistic neomedievalism that applies to Phillips' adaptation of the Benedict poster, if the latter is, in fact, an example of medievalism.[9]

7. For widely available reproductions of Doré's engravings, see *The Doré Illustrations for Dante's Divine Comedy* (New York: Dover, 1976).

8. For more on the innovations of Doré and his engravers, see Claude Bouret, "Doré, ses gravures et ses graveurs," in *Gustave Doré, 1832–1882* (Strasbourg: Musée d'Art Moderne, Cabinet des Estampes, 1983), 207–13.

9. For evidence of Phillips' art-historical sophistication, see his notes and their many references to other artists. Also see Joachim Möller, "Dante, englisch," chap. 8 in *Dantes "Göttliche Komödie": Drucke und Illustrationen aus sechs Jahrhunderten*, ed. Lutz S. Malke (Berlin: Kunstbibliothek, Staatliche Museen zu Berlin, 2000), 153-82, esp. 168–82.

Other challenges in defining Phillips as a stylistic neomedievalist, or, indeed, a neomedievalist of any sort, come to the fore in his parallels to Barry Moser's *Commedia* drawings from the late 1970s and early 1980s.[10] Both artists portray Caiaphas, for example, as if we were crouching at his feet and looking towards his head, rather than standing near his head and looking towards his feet, as Doré depicts him, or seeing him from the side, as Blake portrays him. And both Moser and Phillips center Caiaphas' body, barely include his feet, crop his hands, and leave enough space beyond his head to give a sense of infinite depth. Yet Phillips has left no textual evidence of having seen Moser's illustrations before completing his own, and, as similar as some of their images may be, the parallels could be purely coincidental. Indeed, Dante's play on the Crucifixion in having Caiaphas nailed to the ground strongly invites an ironic echo of looking up at Christ on the cross, and that viewpoint favors: a close view of Caiaphas; the cropping of his extremities; and the suggestion of great space beyond his head. The sheer identification of an artist's immediate influences becomes an obstacle to defining his neomedievalism, particularly in the absence of verbal testimony by him about the sources in question.

Moreover, even if we determine that Moser did indeed influence Phillips, this case exemplifies the challenges of identifying medievalism in possible sources for neomedievalism. Moser often wraps his illustrations around extreme juxtapositions of scale, sharp contrasts in lighting, overt expressions of emotion, and other properties that post-medieval critics sometimes associate with medieval art.[11] But these qualities are invited by Dante's text, are not otherwise lacking in post-medieval art, and are not, in fact, necessarily characteristic of medieval art, or even of Moser's perception of it. That is to say, Moser may not be a medievalist in the sense of a post-medieval artist deliberately playing on medieval principles of art.

Indeed, his style may be more indebted to Neo-gothic art than to that of any other period. Many of his ostensibly medieval qualities were

---

10. For widely available reproductions of Moser's drawings, see Allen Mandelbaum's three-volume translation of the *Commedia* (New York: Bantam, 1982–86; orig. Berkeley: University of California Press, 1980–84).

11. For much more discussion on these characterizations of medieval art, particularly as the latter was seen by Neo-gothic artists and critics, see my "*Commedia* Images in the Neo-Gothic Age(s)," *Studies in Medievalism* 14 (2005), 175–99.

championed by late-eighteenth- and early nineteenth-century critics, and as I have pointed out on other occasions, his work often echoes that of Giovanni Battista Piranesi, Henri Fuseli, and other major artists in the Neo-gothic movement.[12] Thus, his approach to the *Commedia* may incorporate aspects of neomedievalism, and any reference to those aspects by Phillips may qualify as neoneomedievalism, as responses to responses to responses to the Middle Ages.

Phillips' fourth of four illustrations for *Inferno* 22 may also be neo-neomedievalist, as it responds via an intermediary to Blake's third of three illustrations for this canto, but that determination is complicated by ambiguities regarding Blake's relationship to the Middle Ages and regarding the role of the intermediary. Phillips' illustration clearly descends from Blake's, for both images focus on two flying demons about to bump chests over a roiling sea of pitch. Moreover, both artists portray a group of demons gazing towards this foreground clash from the middle ground as Virgil and Dante approach in the distance. And Phillips' figures strike nearly the same poses as their counterparts in Blake's illustration. Yet there are significant differences between the two images. To begin with, Phillips depicts Blake's scene as if it were a panel from a 1940s or 50s comic book: all of the demons have lurid green hair, green wings, and purple bodies; the two colliding demons meet amid a burst of bright yellow above the red word SHOOOOM, which Phillips claims is an inversion of the comic-book expression Woooosh (299); the word THEN and an ellipsis appear in red against a yellow parallelogram in the upper left corner of the image; much of the illustration appears to be formed from small circles that resemble printer's dots in comic books and newspaper illustrations; and the entire image is set within a tan border that, according to Phillips (299), is designed to simulate the yellowing of newspapers and comic books. Moreover, this border extends above Phillips' illustration to embrace a slightly shorter black rectangle in which the two colliding demons are repeated as white outlines flying to the lower right. And the white demon at right is surrounded by a white circle that intersects the frame at four points, while the white demon at left appears just beneath a charcoal-gray rectangle that features cartoon bubbles of text. We are therefore presented with an overtly indebted, yet clearly altered, descendant of Blake's illustration.

12. Those occasions include the 23nd Annual International Conference on Medievalism in Macon, Georgia, and *The Year's Work in Medievalism* 23 (2008).

But we are apparently not presented with an entirely direct response to Blake's illustration, for though Phillips undoubtedly knew the latter, he acknowledges hiring a comic-book illustrator, Paul Tupling, to do the "initial" work of "transcription" (299). Precisely what Tupling did is not clear. And Phillips' use of the terms *initial* and *transcription* would suggest it was not much. Yet the fact that Tupling is a specialist in the format of Phillips' illustration suggests that he may have been responsible for many of the stylistic differences between Phillips' and Blake's interpretations. And that likelihood is reinforced by Phillips' admission that Tupling presented him with a "very well realised basis" for his own image (299). Thus, Phillips was apparently acting as a neoneomedievalist in building his illustration on that of Tupling.

Or was he? Phillips may not, in fact, have been a neoneomedievalist in this case, for Tupling may not have had enough freedom in some regards to qualify as a medievalist. Since he was hired by Phillips, he was presumably constrained by not only his model but also the need to please Phillips. And the fact that Phillips hired him only for this particular "transcription" suggests that Phillips approached Tupling's work with high expectations and kept close tabs on its developments. Indeed, Phillips presumably gave Tupling specific and/or extensive instructions. That is to say, Tupling may have been more an extension of Phillips than an influence on him, and, even in building on Tupling's illustration, Phillips may have been a neomedievalist rather than a neoneomedievalist.

Or he may have been neither, at least to the degree that he directly and/or indirectly responded to Blake's style. Though Blake is undoubtedly a medievalist in the sense that he interpreted a medieval text, he does not necessarily do so in terms that relate to medieval art and/or were perceived by Phillips as doing so. Despite being almost universally acknowledged as a key figure in the Romantic movement, which revolved to some degree around Neo-Gothicism, Blake did not stylistically define himself as a medievalist. In fact, as the art historically well-informed Phillips almost surely knows, Blake's influences incorporate an extraordinarily wide range of sources from almost every preceding period of Western art.[13] And though Phillips claims to have seen a "naive, comic-book aspect"

---

13. Virtually every major study in the massive bibliography on Blake's art at least touches on his myriad sources. For a somewhat dated but highly accessible introduction to that bibliography and to the most overt influences on him, see Kathleen Raine, *William Blake* (London: Thames and Hudson, 1970; repr. 1988).

in Blake's "energetic but rather clumsily realised figures" (299), Phillips seems to be far too current and sophisticated in his thoughts on art history to equate ostensible simplicity or awkwardness with medieval and/or medievalist art. In other words, as he plays off those qualities, he may be neither a neomedievalist nor a neoneomedievalist.

His *Commedia* illustrations thus present myriad versions, blends, offshoots, reflections, and simulacra of neomedievalism, many of which raise issues critical to the definition of not only neomedievalism but also medievalism. They challenge us to refine our distinctions among the ways in which the Middle Ages have been interpreted and to reassess the qualifications, as well as implications, of our evidence. They demonstrate the vitality of our field, even as they call into question its identity and range.

Some Contributions to Middle-earth Lexicography

Hapax Legomena in *The Lord of the Rings*

Jason Fisher

AFTER TOLKIEN HAD FINISHED *The Lord of the Rings*, he wrote to prospective publisher Milton Waldman that "hardly a word in its 600,000 or more has been unconsidered."[1] That is hardly surprising for a work more than a decade in the making, revised and rewritten, both forwards and backwards, many times. Delivering the Valedictory Address to Oxford a few years later, Tolkien said that he "would always rather try to wring the juice out of a single sentence, or explore the implications of one word than try to sum up a period in a lecture, or pot a poet in a paragraph."[2] Tolkien was discussing pedagogy in his address, but in the same letter to Milton Waldman, Tolkien used almost identical wording in reference to his magnum opus: "[i]t is not possible even at great length to 'pot' *The Lord of the Rings* in a paragraph or two."[3] The point is, we should consider ourselves justified in examining sentences, phrases, and even individual words in *The Lord of the Rings*; Tolkien has as good as given us the go ahead.

Moreover, Tolkien himself engaged in this kind of study on many occasions, dealing sometimes with words and phrases from medieval literature, sometimes with words and names of his own invention. It hardly seems necessary to offer a litany of examples to this audience, but to name one—probably the closest analogue to what I will attempt here—there is

---

1. J.R.R. Tolkien, *The Letters of J.R.R. Tolkien*, ed. Humphrey Carpenter (Boston: Houghton Mifflin, 1981), 160.

2. Mary Salu and Robert T. Farrell, eds., J.R.R. Tolkien, *Scholar and Storyteller: Essays in Memoriam* (Ithaca, London: Cornell University Press, 1979), 17.

3. Tolkien, *Letters*, op. cit.

Tolkien's 1925 essay, "Some Contributions to Middle-English Lexicography," from which I have borrowed part of my own title.[4] In some ways, I am also following the model of Tolkien's fellow Inklings, C.S. Lewis and Owen Barfield, whose respective *Studies in Words* and *History in English Words* are concerned to investigate individual words and their interrelationships.[5] If he'd had more free time, it is easy to imagine Tolkien producing a work like those at some point in his career.[6]

With respect to Tolkien's use of words—that is to say, with Tolkien's own literary works as the object of investigation—quite a few essays and word-studies have been published over the years. Perhaps the largest collection of this type is *The Ring of Words*, half a history of Tolkien's lexicographical experience with the *Oxford English Dictionary*, half a collection of word-studies (or perhaps more accurately, one-third, two-thirds). I recommend it highly as a good introduction to the subject. Other scholars who have often explored "the implications of one word" are Tom Shippey, Mark Hooker, J.S. Ryan, and I.[7] But the words I wish to examine in this

---

4. J.R.R. Tolkien, "Some Contributions to Middle-English Lexicography," *RES* 1.2 (April, 1925), 210–215. The first word Tolkien discusses in this essay (a two-word collocation, to be precise) is "long home", in the sense "to depart this life" (210). The *Oxford English Dictionary* had dated the first use of this expression to the first part of the 14th century, but Tolkien notes that his colleague Kenneth Sisam antedated it to the Old English period. Tolkien himself offers a second example, one not yet recorded in the great Bosworth/Toller dictionary and its supplement. Why do I mention this? Because Tolkien himself would go on to use "long home" is this sense twice in the main text of *The Lord of the Rings* (and once in the appendices), making it a dis (or tris) *legomenon* (see note 6, below).

5. C. S. Lewis, *Studies in Words*. 2nd ed. (Cambridge: Cambridge University Press. 1967. [First edition, 1960.]); Owen Barfield, *History in English Words*. Rev. ed. (London: Faber & Faber, 1954. [First edition, Methuen & Co., 1926]).

6. Tolkien provided Lewis with an extended analysis of one particular Indo-European root, intended as raw material for Lewis's *Studies in Words*. Lewis used almost none of it, vexing Tolkien and causing him to label Lewis "at best and worst an Oxford 'classical' don—when dealing with words" (Tolkien, *Letters*, 302). A pity Tolkien never produced his own book on the subject. We know that Tolkien and Lewis planned to collaborate on such a book, though precisely what form it would have taken, had it ever been written, is beyond conjecture. For more on the collaboration that never came to pass, see Steven A. Beebe, "C.S. Lewis on Language and Meaning: Manuscript Fragment Identified," *VII: An Anglo-American Review* 27 (2010), 7–24 (7–8 particularly).

7. An example of each will suffice: Tom Shippey, "History in Words: Tolkien's Ruling Passion," *The Lord of the Rings*, 1954–2004: *Scholarship in Honor of Richard E. Blackwelder*, ed. Wayne G. Hammond and Christina Scull (Milwaukee: Marquette University Press, 2006); Mark T. Hooker, T*he Hobbitonian Anthology of Articles on J.R.R. Tolkien and his Legendarium* (Llyfrawr, 2009); J.S. Ryan, "Before Puck: The Pukel-Men and the

essay are of a particular kind. I would like to consider a few of the *hapax legomena* in *The Lord of the Rings*.

For those who don't normally wield weighty Greek nomenclature with blunt scholarly force, a *hapax legomenon* (ἅπαξ λεγόμενον) is a word that occurs once—and only once—in a written corpus.[8] What kind of corpus we mean depends on the scope of our investigation. We might speak of a word that occurs only once in a particular work, such as *The Lord of the Rings* or the Bible, or a word found only once in an author's entire body of work, such as in Chaucer's or Shakespeare's, or even a word that appears just once in the entire written record of a given language, such as Gothic or Old English.[9] I have no such grand designs in this essay, nor could I possibly discuss all of the *hapax legomena* in just *The Lord of the Rings*, not even in the most cursory fashion because there are more than five thousand of them.

But why discuss them at all? What can we learn by looking at *hapax*es? Naturally, there are many incidental words Tolkien used only once in the novel, the examination of which will may not tell us a great deal—other than attesting to the breadth of the vocabulary at his command. Thus, it isn't particularly interesting to know that Tolkien used only once in *The Lord of the Rings* the words aback, absolute, acrobatics, airless, amble, archery, assistant, auction—and that is just a handful of the A's! Tolkien probably had little or no deliberate intention to limit his use of these words to a single instance. *Hapax legomena* appear in every written corpus. But while most are incidental, some are not. For example, is it worth our notice that there is only one instance of Aman in *The Lord of the Rings*? I think so. In the Second Supplement to the *Oxford English Dictionary*, Robert Burchfield (a protégé of Tolkien's[10]) "emphasized many times (e.g., Vol. 1: xiv) his fondness for inclusion of the *hapax legomena* and eccentric usages of major literary writers ([examples omitted, but

---

Puca," *Mallorn* 20 (1983); Jason Fisher, "Dwarves, Spiders, and Murky Woods: J.R.R. Tolkien's Wonderful Web of Words," *Mythlore* 111/112, Vol. 29 Nos. 1/2 (Fall/Winter 2010).

8. Furthermore, words that occur twice are called *dis legomena*, three times *tris legomena* four *tetrakis*, five *pentakis*, and so on.

9. Tolkien himself has made a few comments on medieval *hapax legomena*. For example, see J.R.R. Tolkien, *Finn and Hengest: The Fragment and the Episode*, ed. Alan Bliss (London: Allen & Unwin, 1982), 89, 95, 112.

10. Christina Scull and Wayne G. Hammond, *The J.R.R. Tolkien Companion and Guide, Volume 2: Reader's Guide* (Boston: Houghton Mifflin, 2006), 142.

Tolkien is footnoted here]). Quite how and why these usages (especially *hapax legomena*) contributed to the language is never made clear, though the analysis would be a valuable one."[11] Such analysis is the subject of this essay (though limited in scope to Tolkien). Burchfield elsewhere refers to such nonce-words as "golden specks in the whole work,"[12] a description which seems apt for the many fascinating *hapax*es salted throughout Tolkien's 600,000-word novel.

When they aren't merely incidental, what sorts of things can we learn from *hapax legomena*? Well, it very much depends what we are looking for, but let me offer a few general observations. These single-use words may call our attention to particular sources, linguistic and literary, from which Tolkien borrowed, as well as give further indications of how he wove them into his work. Or we may learn something about the dialect he used for particular characters when those characters conspicuously employ several *hapax*es. Single occurrences of proper names help to demonstrate the breadth and depth of Tolkien's imagination (though I will not consider proper names in this essay). *Hapax legomena* may even hint at the presence of underlying themes, often deeply buried, but awaiting discovery through lexical analysis. And there is the potential for much more; you never quite know what you're going to find until you start looking.

In this essay I intend to consider a series of *hapax legomena* (or in one case, as noted below, a dis *legomenon*), representing two broad categories of words. The first group includes words drawn from the semi-pagan traditions of the medieval Germanic world. The second has rather the opposite: words with more explicitly Christian connotations. The first will show us something of how Tolkien leaned on his academic training to incorporate pseudo-historical sources into his fiction; the second will spotlight Tolkien's religious faith and reveal some of the traces it left in *The Lord of the Rings*. To put it more concisely: the mortarboard versus the mitre.

---

11. Anthony Paul Cowie, *The Oxford History of English Lexicography*, Volume 1 (Oxford: Oxford University Press, 2009), 270.

12. Robert Burchfield, *Unlocking the English Language*, ([New York]: Hill and Wang, 1991), 12. It may bear noting that it was Burchfield who added Tolkien's own word, hobbit, to the *Oxford English Dictionary* (Second Supplement, Volume 2, 1976).

Medieval Germanic *Hapax Legomena*

As did Barfield and Lewis, let me begin by parading a series of words before you: word-hoard, *weregild, foeman, leechcraft*.[13] What do these words have in common, apart from the most minimal use in *The Lord of the Rings*? The answer is they all derive from the medieval Germanic tradition. Here is the specific context for each of them:

- word-hoard: "Sam leapt to his feet. [. . .] Various reproachful names for himself came to Sam's mind, drawn from the Gaffer's large paternal word-hoard [. . .]."[14]

- *weregild*: "'This I will have as weregild for my father, and my brother,'" he said; and therefore whether we would or no, he took it to treasure it. But soon he was betrayed by it to his death; and so it is named in the North Isildur's Bane [. . .].'"[15]

- foeman: "'[The host] is very great,' said the scout. 'He that flies counts every foeman twice, yet I have spoken to stouthearted men, and I do not doubt that the main strength of the enemy is many times as great as all that we have here.'"[16]

- *leechcraft*: A dis *legomenon*: (1) "[S]aid Théoden [. . .] 'Your *leechcraft* ere long would have had me walking on all fours like a beast;'"[17] (2) "So at last Faramir and Éowyn and Meriadoc were laid in beds in the Houses of Healing; and there they were tended well. For though all lore was in these latter days fallen from its fullness of old, the *leechcraft* of Gondor was still wise, and skilled in the healing of wound and hurt, and all such sickness as east of the Sea mortal men were subject to."[18]

---

13. You will notice that compound words, such as word-hoard, are treated as one. Various analytical rules may be applied to the study of literary corpora. In some cases compounds may be split apart; in other cases, morphological variations may be discounted, treating (for example) say, says, said, etc., as a single "word." The rules may be established to fit the scope and purpose of the research.

14. J.R.R. Tolkien, *The Lord of the Rings*, 50th anniversary ed. (Boston: Houghton Mifflin, 2004), 623 [IV.2]. Considering the proliferation of editions, I have also provided book and chapter hints in this and subsequent quotations from *The Lord of the Rings*.

15. Ibid., 243 [II.2].

16. Ibid., 529 [III.7].

17. Ibid., 519 [III.6].

18. Ibid., 860 [V.8].

Some Contributions to Middle-earth Lexicography

Let us now take these words each in turn and subject them to closer scrutiny.

The first, word-hoard, is perhaps the most conspicuous of the whole group for its evocative sound and prominent figuring in Beowulf —

Him se yldesta   andswarode,
Werodes wísa,   word-hord onléac (ll. 258–9)
(To him the eldest answered,
The leader of the company, his word-hoard unlocked).

The Old English word-hord is, in fact, a *hapax legomenon* in Beowulf, one of many, and the study of such isolated words in that poem has a long and storied past. Even though it may seem to fall into the kind of critical approach that Tolkien warned against, examining the stones and ignoring the tower[19], scholars have greatly profited from such study. Tolkien is quite right that we should admire the beauty and workmanship of the tower, but that does not mean we must never examine the stones out of which it was constructed.[20] So it is with Tolkien's own words. In this case, I have no doubt that Tolkien knew just what he was doing in applying word-hoard to the Gaffer's impressive stock of insults and expletives. Indeed, one of these, "Noodles!", is itself another *hapax* in *The Lord of the Rings*. As with most of the source material underlying the hobbits and their pseudo-history, the intended tone of the allusion is ironic. The Gaffer isn't really like Beowulf. Or maybe he is—if you consider the sharpness of his tongue!

Our next *hapax legomenon*, weregild, is likewise a compound, though usually written without a hyphen. In Old English it is also sometimes spelled wergild, wergeld, or weregeld. It occurs only once in the body of the novel, but if we include the appendices, weregild occurs three times more (from the perspective of the novel and all its paratext, it is a tetrakis *legomenon*). Peter Gilliver, et al., discuss *weregild* in their excellent book *The Rings of Words*,[21] where they quote from the OED definition: "[i]n ancient Teutonic and Old English law, the price set upon a man according to his rank, paid by way of compensation or fine in cases of homicide [...]."

---

19. J.R.R. Tolkien, *The Monsters and the Critics and Other Essays*, ed. Christopher Tolkien (London: Allen & Unwin, 1983), 7–8.

20. Tom Shippey has recently discussed this very subject in "Tolkien's Two Views of Beowulf: One Hailed, One Ignored. But Did We Get This Right?"

21. Peter Gilliver et al., *The Ring of Words: Tolkien and the Oxford English Dictionary* (Oxford: Oxford University Press, 2006), 209–10.

It is composed of the two elements, wer "man" (cp. werewolf) and gild "payment" (cp. yield, guild; and related, gold). Tolkien's choice of this word strikes me as interesting because of the implications it makes about the rule of law in Middle-earth. That is a subject only hinted at, here and there, in *The Lord of the Rings* (as, for example, in Beregond's "trial" for treason). Tolkien's decision to weave a distinctly Germanic legal concept into the fabric of Middle-earth—as opposed to, say, a Roman one—offers us some idea of what jurisprudence in Gondor might have been like.

The Old English form is wergild, but Tolkien adopted the spelling popularized by William Morris in the 19th century. William Morris and Eiríkr Magnússon used the word repeatedly in their translation of the Grettis Saga,[22] a book known to have been in Tolkien's library long before he wrote *The Lord of the Rings*.[23] And in Morris and Magnússon's book, take special note of the back matter, including indexes of "Personal Names," "Local Names," "Things," and "Periphrastic Expressions in the Songs."[24] There is almost an exact analogue, and maybe the actual model, for the indexes of songs, people, places and things Tolkien promised in the first edition of *The Lord of the Rings* and actually delivered in the second.[25]

The next word, *foeman*, is distinctly Anglo-Saxon, with the ring of an arranged marriage between two upstanding English monosyllables, rather the sort of thing George Brewerton must have had in mind when "he demanded this his pupils [at King Edward's School] should use plain old words of the English language" like *muck*.[26] *Foeman* is pure Old

---

22. Morris and Magnússon use *weregild* to translate the Old Icelandic *fégjald* (or simply *gjald*), which is of a slightly different etymology than the Old English *wergild*. The first element of the Norse word is *fé* "cattle; (by metaphoric extension) property, money", cognate to the Old English *feoh*. The second element, *gjald*, is the same as the Old English *gild* "payment". Therefore, the Norse word, even while it means more or less the same as the Old English, lacks the specific etymological implication of a payment or compensation for the life of a man. In the Saga, this sense is usually implied, but Morris and Magnússon introduce it explicitly into their word choice. (Eiríkr Magnússon and William Morris, trans., *Grettis Saga: The Story of Grettir the Strong*, [London: F. S. Ellis, 1869], 283–304). The other common Old Norse word equivalent in meaning to Old English wegild was *baugr*, literally "a ring" (paid as compensation).

23. Scull and Hammond, 601.

24. Magnússon and Morris, 283–304.

25. Morris and Magnússon also include an index of "Proverbs and Proverbial Sayings that Occur in the Story"; Tolkien did not, though some readers might wish he had.

26. Humphrey Carpenter, *Tolkien: A Biography* (Boston: Houghton Mifflin, 1977),

28. Muck is actually Scandinavian. Brewerton should have suggested the native English

English, with its antecedent form, *fáhman*, recorded primarily in Anglo-Saxon law-texts. It is a perfect choice to typify the speech of Rohan, which Tolkien has likened to the ancient English of the Kingdom of Mercia. I could easily spend an entire essay in discussion of such words, many of which are, in fact, *hapax* or *dis legomena* in the novel.[27]

In the interests of brevity, I will limit myself to just one more before leaving the medieval Germanic culture behind: *leechcraft*. This word is used twice in *The Lord of the Rings*, as I pointed out above; furthermore, leech and leeches are each used once, with related meaning. *Leechcraft* refers to the medieval practice of medicine (while leeches, in the sense used by Tolkien, were the practitioners of *leechcraft*; in today's idiom, doctors). The practice of medicine in Anglo-Saxon England—*lǽcecrǽft*—was, to put it euphemistically, not altogether reliable. Many of the healing remedies were no more than folk-medicine, incantations, and in some cases, the actual application of leeches, used to draw out poisons from the blood. Some of these curatives worked well; others might cause more hurt than the illness itself. Tolkien reflects both sides of the medieval medicinal art in the two uses quoted above. Théoden realizes that Gríma's "whisperings," which he likens to *leechcraft*, have caused him great harm. On the other hand, the *leechcraft* of Gondor contributed to the recoveries of Faramir, Éowyn, and Merry after their parts in the Battle of the Pelennor Fields. It may be drawing too great an inference, but I cannot help wondering whether Tolkien chose to use the word exactly twice with the deliberate aim of making this point.

Elements of Religious Truth in Solution

Shifting gears, I would like to consider another series of *hapax legomena* in *The Lord of the Rings*, each of which points, however subtly, to the underlying religious character of the novel. In the Milton Waldman letter,

---

dung, which Tolkien does use in *The Lord of the Rings*, dung and *dunghill* both being *hapax legomena*. For that matter, *muck* (in the compound muck-rakers) is yet another *hapax* legomonen in *The Lord of the Rings*. All of these words occur in the dialogue of orcs—which says a lot about the scatological nature of their idiom.

27. I have discussed this subject in much greater detail elsewhere. For example, see Jason Fisher, "Horns of Dawn: The Tradition of Alliterative Verse in Rohan," *Middle-earth Minstrel: Essays on Music in Tolkien*, ed. Bradford Lee Eden (Jefferson, NC: McFarland, 2010).

once again, Tolkien famously explained his view that myths and fairy-tales must "reflect and contain in solution elements of moral and religious truth (or error), but not explicit, not in the known form of the primary 'real' world"; furthermore, the direct, explicit incorporation of Christianity into these works struck Tolkien as "fatal."[28] A couple of years later, Tolkien (also famously) described his great novel thus: "*The Lord of the Rings* is of course a fundamentally religious and Catholic work; unconsciously so at first, but consciously in the revision. That is why I have not put in, or have cut out, practically all references to anything like 'religion', to cults or practices, in the imaginary world. For the religious element is absorbed into the story and the symbolism."[29]

Taking these two statements together, we should expect to find Christian elements throughout the novel, not overtly, but "in solution"— meaning only in little nods and fillips, carefully hidden away here and there in the greater bulk of the story. What better function for *hapax legomena* than this, to stand in for those elements in solution? There are numerous examples, but I will confine myself to these few: holy, Underworld, hell-hawks, Over-heaven, god. Here is the context of each in *The Lord of the Rings*:

- holy: "The long years have passed like swift draughts of the sweet mead in lofty halls beyond the West, beneath the blue vaults of Varda wherein the stars tremble in the song of her voice, holy and queenly."[30]
- Underworld: "Grond they named it, in memory of the Hammer of the Underworld of old."[31]
- hell-hawks: "'Faramir! The Lord Faramir! It is his call!' cried Beregond. 'Brave heart! But how can he win to the Gate, if these foul hell-hawks have other weapons than fear?"[32]
- Over-heaven: "'The names of all the stars, and of all living things, and the whole history of Middle-earth and Over-heaven and of the

---

28. Tolkien, *Letters*, 144.
29. Ibid., 172.
30. Tolkien, *The Lord of the Rings*, 378 [II.8].
31. Ibid., 828 [V.4].
32. Ibid., 809 [V.4].

Sundering Seas,' laughed Pippin."[33]

- god: "Théoden [...] he was borne up on Snowmane like a god of old, even as Oromë the Great in the battle of the Valar when the world was young."[34]

First, we have holy. The word occurs only once, in Tolkien's translation of the song Galadriel sings to the Fellowship on their departure from Lothlórien. The word translates, in part, the Quenya compound, airetárilírinen ("holy and queenly song"). Tolkien elsewhere explained that airë is "holy," "a title of address to the Valar and the greater Máyar [sic]."[35] The word is here associated with Varda, the Lady of the Stars, Elbereth, whom the Elves revere. Invoked many times by the characters in *The Lord of the Rings*, she is the closest we ever come to a genuine deity in the novel, one who is present and not merely remembered out of a remote past; or if not literally present, she is at least nearby, listening for appeals for aid, and answering them in the darkness.[36]

In the next *hapax*, the Underworld referred to is Angband, the abode of Morgoth in ages past. The word therefore would seem to carry at least as much sense of the pagan as it does of the Cristian Hell. But this is precisely what Tolkien has argued fantasy authors should do: hint at elements of Christian belief without making them explicit. In this case, the Underworld can be regarded a generalized Hell, suitable to Christians

---

33. Ibid., 599 [III.11].
34. Ibid., 838 [V.5].
35. J.R.R. Tolkien, "Words, Phrases, and Passages in Various Tongues in *The Lord of the Rings*," ed. Christopher Gilson, Parma Eldalamberon 17 (2007), 67. At a much earlier stage in the development of Quenya and the legendarium, Tolkien had set down words of a more explicitly religious nature, e.g., *aimo* "saint (m.)," *aire* "saint (f.)," *aimaktu* "martyr," etc. See J.R.R. Tolkien, "The Qenya Lexicon," ed. Christopher Gilson, et al., Parma Eldalamberon 12 (1998), 34. Tolkien is therefore as good as his word in having removed nearly every trace of this from *The Lord of the Rings*—nearly every trace.
36. It is perhaps worth noting here that the word holy is hidden in two words of Tolkien's devising, elsewhere in *The Lord of the Rings*. The first is in Halifirien, a Rohirric place-name which Tolkien has elsewhere glossed as "holy-mount" but which he does not translate in *The Lord of the Rings*; this place-name itself is a *dis legomenon* is the main text of the novel. The second is even more deeply buried, tucked away in Tolkien's appendix on the Shire calendar. There Halimath is given as the Hobbits' name for the ninth month of their calendar. The name is modernized from Old English *háligmónaþ*, "holy-month," a word Tolkien borrowed from Bede's De temporum ratione, from the chapter "De mensibus anglorum." In passing, I should also note that the word holiday is also much used in the Shire, but without any reckoning of its original religious sense.

or pagans alike. But we know that, for Tolkien, this word must also have been a proxy for the literal Hell in which he himself believed. In the next word, Tolkien allows himself to become just a little more direct.

In the compound hell-hawks, Beregond's wonderfully alliterative dysphemism for the winged mounts of the Nazgûl, we have a more explicit reference to Hell. It is true again that Tolkien leaves room for a pseudo-pagan interpretation—even the most superficial knowledge of the medieval Germanic tradition makes that plain, with its many cognates: Old English *hell*, Old Norse *hel*, Old Frisian *helle*, Old Saxon *hellja*, Old High German *hella*, and Gothic *halja*. But all of these words were eventually Christianized, and Tolkien would have been aware that the word had become freighted with Christian overtones. Yet he skirts the edge of explicit reference to religion once again. To use the word more than once would have called too much attention to it; a *hapax legomenon* suited Tolkien's need perfectly.

We find a similar situation with Over-heaven, one of Tolkien's nonce expressions that has always held a special appeal for me. The word heaven, by itself, appears many times in *The Lord of the Rings*, but frequently in the secularized expression, "Good heavens!" The generic noun, heaven(s), appears as well but usually referring merely to the skies or to outer space. Over-heaven is a special case, and as such it deserves the distinction of being used sparingly—in fact, once. In the guide to his nomenclature that Tolkien prepared for translators, he says that Over-heaven is a calque of the Quenya "tar-menel 'high heaven' [...], suggested by ON upphiminn."[37]

The Old Norse term may have been the one on the tip of Tolkien's tongue—the word is conspicuous in the Eddic poem, *Völuspá* (*inter alia*)—but it is hardly unique in the medieval Germanic tradition. In Old High German, *ûfhimil* is itself a *hapax legomenon*, to my knowledge occurring only once in the recorded language, in the late 8th-century *Wessobrunner Schöpfungsgedicht*. There is a cognate form in Old Saxon as well, *uphimil*. As in Old High German, this appears to be a *hapax legomenon* in the language. It occurs at l. 2886 of the great ecclesiastical work, the *Heliand*, in close proximity to *erđa*, "earth," and *uueroldrîki*, "kingdom of the world." In the Old English of Cædmon, there is an even more striking collocation, where we find *middaneard*, *middangeard*, and *upheofon*

---

37. Wayne G. Hammond and Christina Scull, *The Lord of the Rings: A Reader's Companion* (Boston: Houghton Mifflin, 2005), 774.

("over-heaven") all in close proximity. Likewise, the *Völuspá* features both upphiminn and *miðgarðr* in close conjunction.[38]

Clearly, though it may not have been fully taken up into his cosmology, Tolkien felt it very appropriate to drop at least one mention of "over-heaven" into *The Lord of the Rings*. And while there is full support for a pagan reading, it is impossible to ignore the implication that Over-heaven is "the real Heaven," i.e., the Christian Heaven, standing tall above the generalized and secularized uses of "heaven" that otherwise pepper the novel. I might add that it's perfectly appropriate to put this curious *hapax legomenon* into the mouth of the eminently curious Pippin.

And, finally, *god*. Not the singular GOD, written in majuscules. No, Tolkien would not go so far as that (though there is clearly such a singular God in his legendarium, this is beyond the scope of *The Lord of the Rings*). This is "a god," one of many; moreover, this god is rendered less significant through the miniscule spelling and made more remote through the use of simile: Théoden is "like a god of old" (emphasis added). There are no actual gods overseeing the battlefield; this is not *The Iliad*. Yet an actual god is named in this passage, Oromë the Hunter. This is one of only a few explicit references to the Valar (excepting the frequent invocations to Elbereth), and it is the only one to use the word god. Tolkien has been very careful indeed to avoid the word heretofore,[39] and he will not use it

---

38. Tolkien's expertise in Old Norse is beyond question. The fact that he referred to the Old Norse word upphiminn in his own notes for translators is sufficient proof, and there is ample further evidence, not least of which is Tolkien explicit acknowledgements that he drew the names of his Dwarves and Gandalf from the Völuspá. Tolkien's knowledge of Old High German and Old Saxon, perhaps, requires a word or two of justification. For proof of Old High German, see J.R.R. Tolkien, "Philology: General Works," *The Year's Work in English Studies* 4 (1923), 24, and J.R.R. Tolkien, "Philology: General Works," *The Year's Work in English Studies* 6 (1925), 39, *inter alia*. The proof of Old Saxon is even more compelling. In "Philology: General Works" (1923), Tolkien discusses the *Heliand* with special reference to the word heƀanriki, "kingdom of heaven," and its proper rendering in Old English (35). This word is very close in sense to *uphimil* and *uueroldriki*. In "Philology: General Works" (1925), Tolkien favorably reviews a new dictionary of Old Saxon, E.H. Sebrt's *Vollständiges Wörterbuch zum Heliand und zur Altsächsischen Genesis*, and compares it to another (57).

39. Two variations on god—one a *hapax*, the other a dis *legomenon* in *The Lord of the Rings*—might be mentioned here: lor and lawks, in Tolkien, *The Lord of the Rings*, 63 [I.2], 102 [I.V]. Lor is a reference to the Lord, i.e., to God, but by softening it to the dialectal form, Tolkien attenuates any religious significance, reducing it to another "element in solution." Likewise, the interjection Lawks is an alteration of Lord. By using a colloquial form, and only once in more than half a million words, the hint of any

again, so why here, why in that instance? The answer is probably that the image of Théoden's arrival at Minas Tirith represents the focal center of the power and majesty of the entire War of the Ring. This is the moment at which a culture struggling to survive in the face of overwhelming evil would have the greatest need for God, and Tolkien gives us just a taste. This the moment of greatest jeopardy and fear,[40] and Tolkien writes just enough—not one letter more!—to suggest the appeal to faith in a higher power. The balance Tolkien has struck is perfect. To me the closing paragraph of "The Ride of the Rohirrim" is one of the most powerful passages in all of Tolkien's writings.

A Closing Remark

Not every *hapax legomenon* is significant. Every written corpus has them, from the shortest story to the longest epic, and many are quite ordinary words of limited individual importance. Likewise, the words used most often are usually not significant (the, and, of . . .). It would be supposing too much to take every *hapax* as a conscious and deliberate clue to readers, even by a wordsmith as meticulous as Tolkien. Yet surely some of them were deliberate attempts to dissolve important themes and sources "in solution" in Tolkien's great work. I have tried to demonstrate (albeit briefly) that one can learn quite a bit from the small things; the lessons *hapax*es can teach us are often disproportionately greater than the words themselves or their places in the larger work. And having pulled a few needles out of the haystack, I hope to see much further study of Tolkien's many *hapax* and *dis legomena*. The devil is in the details, the old saw goes, and a single word out of 600,000 is quite a detail in which to hide a devil—or a god.

---

religious undertone is once again, so much subtler.

40. At the macroscopic level. At the microscopic level, this instance is counterbalanced by the test of Frodo and Sam's faith on the journey to Mordor, by the jeopardy and fear they face at Torech Ungol, and by the spirit-crushing march to Mount Doom. A lesser author than Tolkien would have been tempted to place an explicit appeal to God in the mouths of Frodo and Sam, but Tolkien is more careful. There are invocations, but they are made through glossolalia (a religious miracle)—and they remain untranslated and inexplicit.

The *World of Warcraft*

A Medievalist Perspective

Simon Roffey

Introduction

THE MEDIEVAL PERIOD HAS long been a source of inspiration for the creation of imaginary and fantasy worlds. Scholars of medievalism have investigated how the Middle Ages has informed a range of genres and media, from traditional art and literary forms to more contemporary culture such as film, music and, more recently, digital media. In the last few years computer games have outsold music and video combined. In 2008 spending on games had an estimated rise of 42 percent to £4.64 billion pounds as compared to sales on music and video at £4.46 billion pounds. Like it or not, gaming is hugely popular and potentially offers widespread access to a variety of medievalist themes and ideas. Massively Multiplayer Online Roleplaying Games (MMORPGs),[1] such as Blizzard's *World of Warcraft*,[2] offer regular interactive access to diverse and populated worlds many of which carry medieval themes. These games, including titles such as *Lord of the Rings Online* and *Dark Age of Camelot*, derive their world structure, places, buildings and artifacts from the medieval period as well as aspects of lore, mythology and storyline.[3] *World of Warcraft*, the world's

---

1. MMORPGs are online games that involve a large amount of players. The game worlds themselves are often "persistent" in that they can evolve and change even when players are offline.

2. Blizzard Entertainment (2004).

3. Medievalism's influence on games is of course not limited to online PC games.

highest populated online game, has attracted over 11.5 million subscriptions worldwide, a far higher number, for example, than currently study medieval history at the undergraduate level.[4] Importantly, among a profusion of RPG computer games with relatively short life spans, *World of Warcraft* has retained its popularity since its release in late 2004. As such it has become the standard by which other MMORPGs are judged.[5]

The academic study of computer games has long been the preserve of digital media studies and social and anthropological scholarship.[6] Furthermore, despite medievalism being an apparent "movement in general culture,"[7] its relationship to forms of digital media as popular culture, such as music, popular writing, and games has received little attention when compared to more traditional or classic forms of so-called higher culture. This deficit has however been recently addressed somewhat.[8] In particular the 2008 edition of *Studies in Medievalism* focussed on the use of the medieval past in old and new technology and featured a series of papers that examined the influence of the medieval period on modern role-playing computer games. These essays comprised an examination of historical elements in computer role-playing games, with particular emphasis on

---

Console games, in particular, for the Xbox and Playstation 3 have comparative games. Among the the most popular are the traditional fantasy-based rpg *The Elder Scrolls: Oblivion* (Bethesda), *Dragon Age* (Bioware) and the *Assassin's Creed* series (Ubisoft), where the action largely takes in fairly accurate reconstructions of medieval cities including Jerusalem and Florence.

4. 2008/2009 figures http://us.blizzard.com/en-us/company/press/pressreleases.html?081121, accessed 30 May 2011.

5. Even the the more traditional areas of the media were quick to jump on the game's popularity. In 2007 The *Times* newspaper offered a free 14-day *World of Warcraft* trial and an associated eight-page supplement.http://technology.timesonline.co.uk/tol/news/tech_and_web/gadgets_and_gaming/article1551545.ece, accessed 28 June 2010

6. Important general studies include those of Brad King and John Borland, *Dungeons and Dreamers: the Rise of Computer Game Culture from Geek to Chic*, (New York: Mc-Graw Hill and Osborne, 2003), Frans Mayra, ed., *Computer Games and Digital Cultures: Conference Proceedings* (Tampere: Tampere University Press, 2002), Edward Castronova, *Synthetic Worlds: The Business and Culture of Online Games*, (University of Chicago Press, 2005), and T.L. Taylor, *Play Between Worlds* (Cambridge, MA: The MIT Press 2006).

7. Michael Alexander, *Medievalism: The Middle Ages in Modern England* (London: Yale University Press, 2007), xxviii.

8. See Eddo Stern "A Touch of the Medieval: Narrative, Magic and Computer Technology in Massively Multiplayer Computer Role-Playing Games," (2002), http://ic.media.mit.edu/courses/mas878/pubs/stern-cgdc02-touch-of-medieval.pdf, Accessed July 1, 2010.

Knights of the Temple and the MMORPG *Dark Age of Camelot*, as well as a theoretical reflection on perceptions of gender. These papers highlighted the important relationship between digital games and a pseudo-medieval past[9] and the wider social implications, particularly with regard to perceptions of gender.[10] As one author notes, RPG games, aside from strategy games, may represent the "most prominent category of computer games containing such themes."[11] *World of Warcraft* itself has been the subject of numerous academic articles and books exploring a range of diverse issues including capitalism, death, religion, myth, addiction, gender and philosophy.[12] However, as of yet, the game has surprisingly received comparatively little attention in the field of medievalism, despite its unprecedented popularity and diverse and long-standing player base.[13]

This article will therefore consider the use of medieval themes in *World of Warcraft* and their relevance to the studies in medievalism. Consequently it will argue that such references can be grouped into two major forms: *Generic reference,* which draws upon a broad palette of pseudo-medieval ideas; *Direct reference*, which draws example from specific identifiable features of the medieval past. Overall it will not argue whether the veracity and realism of such representation is important, but rather why it is useful in providing a creative and coherent framework in which

9. Carol L. Robinson, "An Introduction to Medievalist Games," *Studies in Medievalism XVI: Medievalism in Technology Old and New* (2008), 123-25; Oliver M. Traxel, "Medieval and Pseudo-Medieval Elements in Computer Role-Playing Games: Use and Interactivity," *Studies in Medievalism XVI: Medievalism in Technology Old and New* (2008), 125-43.

10. Amy S. Kaufman, "Romancing the Game: Magic, Writing, and the Feminine in Neverwinter Nights," *Studies in Medievalism XVI: Medievalism in Technology Old and New* (2008), 143–59; Lauryn S. Mayer, "Promises of Monsters: The Rethinking of Gender in MMORPGs," *Studies in Medievalism XVI*, 184–205.

11. Traxel, "Medieval and Pseudo-Medieval Elements in Computer Role-Playing Games," 127.

12. Hilde G. Corneliussen and Jill Walker Rettberg, eds., *Digital Culture, Play, and Identity: A World of Warcraft Reader* (Cambridge, MA: The MIT Press 2008); William Sims Bainbridge, *The Warcraft Civilization: Social Science in a Virtual World* (Cambridge, MA: The MIT Press 2010); Luke Cuddy and John Nordlinger (eds.), *World of Warcraft and Philosophy* (Illinois: Open Court 2009).

13. Hilde G. Corneliussen and Jill Walker Rettberg, "Introduction: 'Orc Professor LFG,' or Researching in Azeroth" in Corneliussen and Rettberg, eds., pages 1–17, 7. Over the last few years a series of papers have been given on the subject at the International Conference on Medievalism including Nancy Heckel, "10 Million and Growing OR What Medievalists Should Know About *World of Warcraft*" (2008).

the game content can emerge. Ultimately it will consider the importance of using such media for the widespread portrayal of medieval themes in providing a creative context for the exploration of a reconstituted medieval past.[14]

A Short History of MMORPGS[15]

The origins of computer role-playing games lie in the popular pen and paper version, *Dungeons and Dragons* (D&D), created by Gary Gygax and Richard Arneson in the early 1970s.[16] The influence of this game on the late computer versions cannot be overstated.[17] Indeed later PC game developers such as Richard Garriott, creator of the hugely popular *Ultima* series, and Chris Metzen of *World of Warcraft*, were themselves formerly long-term *Dungeons and Dragons* players.[18] The relationship between *D&D* and the medieval period has been already discussed by Schick and by Marshall, who comments that the medieval period forms an important "ingredient repository" for such game worlds.[19]

Garriott himself was responsible for creating one of the first commercially published computer roleplaying games, *Akalabeth: World of Doom* in 1979.[20] The game, which takes its name from a story in Tolkien's *Silmarillion* collection, contained most of the core elements recognized in today's RPGs and MMORPGs, such as character classes, experience

---

14. From my own experience, new archaeology students are now more likely to have been exposed to medieval themes through music and computer games than through books or popular TV programs.

15. A competent history of MMORPGs has been previously discussed by Mayer, "Promises of Monsters." However, it is useful here to consider such developments in relation to *World of Warcraft*.

16. *Dungeons and Dragons* (TSR, 1974).

17. King and Borland, *Dungeons and Dreamers*, page 4.

18. Interview with Richard Garriot in 1997 http://uk.gamespot.com/features/ultima/g1.html, accessed 30 June 2010; Interview with Chris Metzen http://www.gamesradar.com/f/the-history-of-warcraft/a-20100203949 50782059 Accessed 30 June 2010.

19. Lawrence Schick, *Heroic Worlds: A History and Guide to Role-Playing Games* (New York: Prometheus Books, 1991), 14; David W. Marshall, "A World unto Itself: Autopoietic Systems and Secondary Worlds in *Dungeons and Dragons*," in David W. Marshall, ed., *Mass Market Medieval: Essays on the Middle Ages in Popular Culture*, (Jefferson and London: McFarland, 2007), 171.

20. Matt Barton *Dungeons and Desktops: The History of Computer Roleplaying Games*, (Wellesley, MA: AK Peters Ltd 2008), 1.

leveling and attributes. As a result of the popularity of *D&D*, and the later *Advanced Dungeons and Dragons* (*AD&D*), the 1980s and early 1990s witnessed the introduction of a range of fantasy RPG games. Despite presenting comparatively different game content in the form of world construction and story, these games derived their structure from a shared medieval-type framework and environment. Among these were the *AD&D Forgotten Realms* series initially with *Pools of Radiance* (1988) followed by the *Eye of the Beholder* (1990) and the AOL online game *AD&D Neverwinter Nights* (1991), the first graphical MMORPG.[21] 1994 saw the release of influential *Elder Scrolls* series, the second title of which, *Daggerfall*, presented the largest explorable world to date, a land mass that was claimed to be more than double that of Britain.[22]

In 1996 *Meridian 59* became the first truly massively multiplayer online RPG game that also introduced the monthly subscription, now a fairly standard practice in today's MMORPGs.[23] A year later saw the release of Garriott's *Ultima Online*[24] series, a game that is credited with popularizing the genre. The mid-late 1990s and early 2000s witnessed the introduction of a range of fantasy-based RPG games[25] that presented more "free-ranging, creative and sprawling environments"[26] and also capitalized on opportunities presented for greater online multiplayer contexts.[27] One such game was *Dark Age of Camelot* (2001),[28] which had clear associations with a perceived sub Romano-British "Dark Age" and Arthurian legend. Tolkien's *Lord of Rings* (1954; 1955) has long provided important source material for the more fantastical elements of RPG games; it appeared in MMORPG form as *Lord of the Rings Online* in 2007.

21. *Pools of Radiance* (Strategic Simulations Inc.,1988); *Eye of the Beholder* (Strategic Simulations Inc.,1990) and *AD&D Neverwinter Nights* (Stormfront Studios, 1991).

22. *ElderScrolls II: Daggerfall*, (Bethesda,1996); http://www.bethsoft.com/eng/games/games_daggerfall.html, Accessed 4 May 2010.

23. *Meridian 59* (Archetype Interactive, 1996).

24. *Ultima Online* (Origins Systems / EA, 1997).

25. This period also saw the release of the strategy games series developed by The Creative Assembly including *Total War* (2000) with *Medieval: Total War* and *Rome: Total War* following soon after (2002; 2004).

26. Kaufman in *Studies in Medievalism XVI*, 143.

27. Popular games include *Everquest* (Sony, 1999), *Guild Wars* (ArenaNet, 2005), *Dungeons and Dragons Online* (Turbine, 2006), *Age of Conan* (Funcom, 2008) and *Warhammer Online* (Mythic Entertainment, 2008).

28. *Dark Age of Camelot* (Mythic Entertainment, 2001)

The period also witnessed a proliferation of PC RPG games including Bioware's *Neverwinter Nights* (2002), *Elder Scrolls: Oblivion* (2006), and *Dragon Age: Origins* (2009) among many others. *World of Warcraft* itself appeared in its current online form in 2004, having initially appeared as a single and multiplayer PC game in 1994 entitled simply *Warcraft: Orcs and Humans*.[29] This game was originally closer to a strategy-based game than a traditional RPG, and whilst its mechanics and gameplay lacked the diversity and complexity of its later successors, it nonetheless provided the basis from which the later games would emerge.[30]

Methodology: an archaeological investigation

Before we consider some of the medieval aspects of *Warcraft*'s world of Azeroth, a brief discussion concerning the methods of data collection should first be examined, since research in a virtual world requires a unique approach. However unconventional this particular research seems, one should note that it is not the first of it type. Many who have so far traversed Azeroth in the name of research include the sociologist Bainbridge who spent more than 2,300 hours and a number of characters conducting an "ethnographic participant observation" of the world, the results of which were published as a book.[31] In January 2006 an online guild for academics, the Truants, was set up specifically to support research on *World of Warcraft*.[32] Two years later an idea by John Bohannon led to the holding of a series of in-game virtual academic conferences.[33] In 2008 the game designer James Wallis conducted a "geophysical survey" of the continents of Azeroth, Kalimdor and the Eastern Kingdoms. His aim

---

29. *Warcraft: Orcs and Humans* (Blizzard Entertainment, 1994); *Neverwinter Nights* (Bioware, 2002); *World of Warcraft* (Blizzard Entertainment, 2004); *Elder Scrolls: Oblivion* (Bethesda, 2006); *Dragon Age Origins* (Bioware, 2009).

30. The game also inspired a series of novels. The first Warcraft novel, *Day of the Dragon*, written by Richard Knaak, was published in 2001 (New York: Pocket Books). The game has also attracted the attention of the film industry and a film directed by Sam Raimi is currently in production (2010).

31. Bainbridge, *The Warcraft Civilization*, 15.

32. Corneliussen and Jill Walker Rettberg, "Introduction," 7.

33. John Bohannon, "Slaying Monsters For Science," *Science 320*, (2008), http://www.sciencemag.org/cgi/content/full/320/5883/1592c. Accessed 2 July 2010; Bainbridge, *The Warcraft Civilization*, 16.

was to measure the size and density of the world, and he calculated that the total land mass of the Azeroth at this time was 113 square kilometres.[34]

This research was conducted between 2009 and 2010 and involved the use of a range of low and high level characters.[35] The data collection took the form of a survey undertaken individually and as part of groups undertaking quests, instances and raids. The survey itself comprised the examination of various buildings and features with reference to medieval examples. Screenshots were taken of over 130 features and used as a photographic database from which comparisons could be made with real examples. What was clear overall was that, although there were some direct examples, the majority were largely generic and non-specific but nonetheless comprised features which were clearly based on general medieval conventions.

The *World of Warcraft*

World of Warcraft is set in the world of Azeroth. As well as humans, the world is the home of a number of diverse races, some that are instantly recognizable from other medieval-based fantasy genres including dwarves, elves, orcs, trolls, and the undead. There are also races that are largely unique to the game: the tauren, based on the classical minotaur, and draenai. The races comprise two main player-factions, the Alliance, and its counterpart, the Horde, with a common non-player enemy in the Scourge and Burning Legion.[36] As in other MMORPGs players create a character, choosing its race, faction, and class. The latter includes the standard fantasy fare including warriors, mages, priests, shamans, druids and rogues. Primary and secondary professions can also be learnt and developed, through the game and these diverse crafts include leather-working, alchemy, fishing, cookery, jewel-cutting, and engineering.[37] Players develop, or level, their characters through a range of in-game experiences

---

34. http://www.guardian.co.uk/technology/video/2008/jun/25/interesting.world.warcraft. Accessed 15 May 2010.

35. Some areas of the world could only be unlocked by characters of a certain level. Outland, for example, could only be accessed via a character of level 58 or higher.

36. http://www.wowwiki.com/Azeroth_%28world%29. Accessed 30 June 2010.

37. The recent Cataclysm expansion, sees the introduction of the archaeologist secondary profession http://www.wow.com/2009/08/21/blizzcon-2009-archaeology-and-path-of-the-titans/. Accessed 4 May 2011.

including exploration, quests, and closed-dungeons instances. Players can also progress their characters through pvp play (player versus player) and small- and large-scale raids. The world where the action takes place is detailed and expansive and contains a wide variety of environments from icy wastelands through to rainforest, tundra, mountains, farms, villages, and settlements. The cities contain a diverse urban make-up comprising quasi-micro economies of trade, shops, auctions, and banks. The *World of Warcraft* presents a complex world indeed.

However, its history, or lore, gives the world meaning and a sense of a place in time. Here *World of Warcraft* truly excels with a chronology that stretches back millennia and is sufficiently detailed to provide a comprehensive "ideas repository" for game content. This history is often revealed piece-meal via conversations, quests, instances, and chance findings, as well as a library of novels, guides, and related online resources.[38] *World of Warcraft* thus presents an intricate world, a world of fantasy, albeit one that is pure medievalism in its lore, structure, and society.

Fantasy and Medievalism

Like many RPG games, *World of Warcraft* derives much of its inherent architecture and content directly from literary works of fantasy, which themselves draw inspiration from the medieval period. Krzywinska has noted that these essentially fictional worlds, created by writers such as Robert Howard and J. R. R. Tolkien, act as a "blue print formulation" which are then used and extended.[39] These, in turn, are derived from "pre-existing mythological cosmologies" including Arthurian, Celtic, and Nordic traditions.[40] Certainly the underlying myths or lore prevalent with *World of Warcraft* draw heavily upon pre-existing myth, and these signifiers of a prehistoric and historic past help provide the "illusion of a coherent world."[41] In the case of *World of Warcraft* this lore, woven with

---

38. Popular external sites include http://www.wowwiki.com; http://www.wow.al-lakhazam.com, and http://thottbot.com. Accessed 4 May 2011. Increasingly there are also a range of podcasts, soundtracks and Iphone Apps that relate to the lore of *World of Warcraft*.

39. Tanya Krzywinska, "World Creation and Lore: *World of Warcraft* as Rich Text," in Corneliussen and Rettberg, eds.,123–43, (125).

40. Krzywinska "World Creation and Lore", 125.

41. Krzywinska "World Creation and Lore", 125.

myths as "complex as anything found in the ancient sagas," has led to one author to go so far as to claim the game a virtual "civilisation."[42]

In *World of Warcraft* these myths are often recognisable both within elements of story and also in the personal names of some of the characters, for example the Huscarls from the Howling Fjord and Drottin Hrothgar, from Hrothgar's Landing, which pays reference to the Danish king in the epic poem *Beowulf*. In particular, Arthurian myths feature in the game, introduced originally in the non-rpg versions and explored more fully in the 2008 expansion *World of Warcraft: Wrath of the Lich King*. One the main villains or bosses, in this expansion, and from whose actions the central story revolves, is Arthas, the Lich King. Arthas, whose mentors are the aptly named Uther and Muradin, is an antithetical Arthur whose fate as the king likewise begins with the drawing of the sword, Frostmourne, from the ice. This story provides much of the content for the expansion in the form of quests and instances and the inevitable end game where players confront the Lich King and claim the sword for themselves. In this way the players become part of a dynamic lore.

The game content of the Lich King expansion also draws heavily on Nordic Mythology, in particular early medieval prose and the poetic Eddas. Here much of the action takes place in the frozen north lands of Northrend where dwell the Vrykul, a people who bear close similarity to Vikings and perhaps more specifically to the Einherjar, or dead heroes, of the Norse medieval Eddas. The Vrykul are also linked along with the Val'kyr, who serve the same role as the Valkyries, albeit malignly. The creation of Azeroth by the so-called Titans also pays reference to Norse mythology. Here, the two Titan Pantheons, Aesir and Vanir, or storm and earth, respectively, are references to the pantheons of Gods in Norse myth, the Æsir and the Vanir. The Titan Watchers of Azeroth, Loken, Thorim, Freya, Hodir and Mimiron, are likewise based on the gods Loki, Thor, Freyja, Hod, and Mimir, respectively, and their stories and backgrounds are all fairly similar. Moreover, aspects of Norse myth can be found elsewhere in Azeroth particularly within the lore of the elves, for example. The damaged great world tree, Nordrassil, is the Norse Yggdrasil. Furthermore, just as the god Odin sacrificed himself on Yggdrasil,[43] likewise the bones of the demon assailant Archimonde hang from its

---

42. Bainbridge, *The Warcraft Civilization*, 14.

43. Carolyne Harrington (trans.), *The Poetic Edda* (Oxford: Oxford University Press, 1999), 34.

virtual counterpart.⁴⁴ Importantly, and somewhat surprisingly perhaps, this lore or history is not static but is subject to "historical shifts."⁴⁵ One example of this occurred on 10 November 2008. This day witnessed the invasion of Stormwind City and its Horde counterpart, Orgrimmar, by the forces of Arthas. A result of this attack was the launch of a reprisal by Alliance and Horde forces on Northrend, an expedition which opened up the continent for player exploration (and therefore the game's expansion).

The physical context for the story is a world replete with diverse environments and societies, buildings and people. These environments span over three main continents or lands: Kalimdor, Northrend, and the Eastern Kingdoms, as well as Outland, accessed through the Dark Portal.⁴⁶ These continents contain zones and regions.⁴⁷ In the Eastern Kingdoms, a continent distinctly reminiscent of medieval Europe, can be found the somewhat familiar shires, such as Northshire and Goldshire. Here the constructed world, often beautifully and imaginatively rendered, supplies an apt environment for the story. In a sense it acts as an "extended imaginary terrain" that either "intersects with the real world" or provides a mixture of familiar and unfamiliar geographical features.⁴⁸ Importantly, the game environment provides a physical presence for aspects of the lore presented mainly through the textual information of quests. At times this form of history can be supported by archaeological examples, presented by the ruins of temples and great cities, such as Lordaeron. In this once great city, the blood-spattered throne room bears physical testament to the traitorous murder of its last king. However, whilst the lore is crucial to the story that drives much of the game, arguably the immersive physical environment itself both holds the attention and provides the context in which the action takes place. Indeed as one of the game's senior designer's has recently noted, stories are often communicated through gameplay and use of visuals and not always through the text.⁴⁹

44. http://www.wowwiki.com/Nordrassil. Accessed 1 July 2010.

45. Bainbridge, *The Warcraft Civilization*, page 14. Various films of the event were recorded and can be found at http://www.youtube.com/watch?v=BAVJz78U_oM. Accessed 1 July 2010.

46. There are also several smaller islands, such as Teldrassil, home of the Night Elves

47. An interactive map of the world and its zones and regions can be found at http://mapwow.com. Accessed 1 July 2010.

48. Krzywinska "World Creation and Lore," 137.

49. Josh Augustine, "The Stories behind the Stories," *World of Warcraft Official*

The Medieval *World of Warcraft*

Medievalism is present throughout all of Azeroth, not just in the monuments and buildings, but also in the fashions, weapons, trades, and crafts. Medieval-type institutions are represented perhaps more directly through the player guilds, which bear marked similarities with late medieval fraternities. However, in the buildings and physical features of Azeroth we most strongly see the influence of medievalism. The influence is apparent in two main form: direct, drawing from real examples or specific types, and generic in that influences are derived from a broader palette of medieval ideas and themes.

World of Warcraft's history stretches back some 10,000 years, a past revealed by the game's evolving storyline and lore but also distinctly visible in the crumbling, but once sumptuous monuments that litter the game world environment. These relics of ancient civilization marked by ruinous temples and deserted castles and villages lend a leitmotif of mystery and nostalgia, in which the context of the game is given both atmosphere and drama. This includes the recent addition of the Halls of Origination, an Egyptian-influenced lost temple complex replete with pharaohs, pyramids, and obelisks. In turn the synthesis of past and present suggests a fragile world in transition beset by conflict and instability in which new nations and societies find their place and strive for survival. In this sense this world parallels that of early medieval Europe after the fall of Rome. In Azeroth one gets a sense of further impending upheaval, and relationships between past and present become more acute as the game enters its *Cataclysm* expansion.[50]

In *World of Warcraft* we can see a range of medieval influences on the architecture, form, and fabric of Azeroth's built environment, as well as arts, crafts, trades, weapons, and armor, many with clear medieval precedents. The visual aspects of the world are beautifully rendered by teams of specialist designers and artists, a fact that has not gone unnoticed in more mainstream media. A recent *Guardian* article compared the "glorious space" of the game to a "work of art" that is "as glorious as Chartres" and, importantly, presents a "communal experience of culture."[51] To

---

Magazine (2010), 12, 9-17.

50. The Cataclysm leads to dramatic environmental changes to areas of Azeroth. Many areas become ruinous.

51. Sam Leith, "The *World of Warcraft* Video Game is Every Bit as Glorious as Chartres

some, that may be hyperbolic license, but whatever the aesthetic value of *Warcraft*'s art, it is significantly attractive to millions of people of all ages and social backgrounds. And, through its rendition of more identifiable works of art, for example via the architecture and decorative detail of its cathedrals and monumental buildings, it pays clear reference to medieval art forms, from the ruinous Byzantine majesty of Lordaeron to the timber-framed buildings of the Elwyn Forest and Tirisfal Glades.

The reference to medievalism is particularly noticeable with the religious buildings of the Eastern Kingdoms, such as Northshire Abbey, the Scarlet Monastery, and the great Cathedral of Stormwind City. The overall style of Azeroth's ecclesiastical architecture is distinctly medieval European with stylized traces of both late Romanesque and early gothic styles of the eleventh and twelfth centuries. This influence appears in Stormwind's Cathedral of Light, for example. Here the great vaulted processional nave of the cathedral is flanked by rib-vaulted aisles and terminates in an apsidal raised chancel with glazed lancet windows. The walls of the cathedral, like similar examples, is largely devoid of decoration, however. There is no overt religious iconography in Azeroth's cathedrals and churches. Bare walls and floors are sometimes decorated by the plain tapestries, carpets, and symmetrical tiles. No religious icons adorn the "altars," which themselves are often represented by plain tables, sometimes holding an open book on a subject of history or philosophy. In some ways, Azeroth's churches are similar to their medieval counterparts, both in an institutional sense, e.g., building types, bishops and priests (Benedictus is the current Archbishop), and military orders, and in an ideological sense, with their emphasis on preaching and education as well as adherence to the three Virtues of Respect, Tenacity, and Compassion. In the lack of decoration and overt religious symbolism, however, the churches and cathedrals of Azeroth differ greatly from their real counterparts. Medieval churches were often replete with religious icons and imagery formed in worship to the Christian God. However, in Azeroth, the Church of the Holy Light is presented as a non-theistic philosophical ideology, and within this almost secular religion there is no requirement for ritualized and symbolic icons and imagery. In terms of real religion, Blizzard plays it safe.

Cathedral," http://www.guardian.co.uk/technology/2009/nov/29/world-of-warcraft-sam-leith. Accessed 1 July 2010.

The Church of the Holy Light is not proliferate but once had a number of monasteries, temples, and churches scattered across the lands. Many were destroyed in the so-called Third War, but some do survive in part, including part of Northshire Abbey, the Scarlet Monastery (now overtaken by a fanatical militant order, the Scarlet Crusade), and a small number of churches. These small churches are not numerous but include Light's Hope Chapel in the Eastern Plaguelands and the largely deserted chapels outside Karazhan in Deadwind Pass, Kiri'nVar, Netherstorm, and Deathknell in Tirisfal Glades. These chapels all conform to a specific architectural form: a simple, single cell structures with squat western towers of the type commonly found in western Europe between the tenth and twelfth centuries. Interestingly, the masonry towers of Azeroth churches are decorated with vertical pilaster strips. This structural arrangement, which almost gives the impression that the tower is of timber construction, can be compared to Anglo-Saxon examples in England such as Barton on Humber (Humberside), Sulgrave (Northamptonshire), and Earls Barton (Northamptonshire).

Monasteries were formerly an important institution within the Church of Holy Light. The best surviving example is the Scarlet Monastery located in the north of the Eastern Kingdoms and not far from the once-great alliance city of Lordaeron. The monastery conforms to the late medieval layout of formally arranged church with attached cloister. The church itself is of particular architectural note in that its twin decorated spires resemble those of the twelfth-century cathedral of Chartres and particularly those of Cologne Cathedral (founded in the mid-thirteenth century). Significantly those at Cologne were a work of neo-medievalism themselves, being constructed in the nineteenth century.

The often lush and dramatic landscapes of Azeroth littered with castles, forts and outposts. Unsurprisingly the masonry castles of the Eastern Kingdoms are monumental edifices replete with bastions, embattlements, and barbicans. The encircling walls of the port and castle as Stormwind contain the town and cathedral, parks, gardens, and the defensive keep. On the west side is the bustling port. The castles of the Eastern Kingdoms, such as Wintergarde Keep (Dragonblight), Theramore Keep (the only heavily fortified Alliance outpost in Kalimdor), and the now deserted Stromgarde Keep (Arathi Highlands) reflect a world that is at almost constant war.[52] As such (both in design, style, and at time locations[53]) they draw upon the architectural heritage of their late medieval European counterparts such as Gisors and Carcassonne, France, and English/Welsh castles at Conwy, Caernarvon, and Pembroke, for example. Like these latter examples, both Stormwind and to a greater extent Theremore rely on their coastal location, both for supplies and for reinforcements. Other castles, operating more in terms of strategic outposts, such as Nethergarde Keep, located so as to guard the Dark Portal, an access point from the world of Outland, and Fordragon Hold, Dragonblight, which besieges Arthas's Icecrown Citadel, are often located in hills or mountainsides or placed on promontories. Here they are well placed for strategic purposes and loose parallels can perhaps be found in the Crusader castles, such as Kerak and Krak de Chevalier, Syria. In England, castles at Richmond, North Yorkshire, and Corfe, Dorset, were positioned so as to protect important communication routes. The layout of Azeroth's castles is naturally stylized and generic, reflecting the required components and settings that best fit the unfolding stories and quests as well as adding a sense of drama. These generic features include battlements, bastions and drawbridges. Most castles contain an outer work (bailey) with a central keep, and the entrance to Stormwind is via a barbican similar to that found at the French Chateau Gaillard, for example.

Castles, churches, and monasteries are perhaps among the most typical of medievalist structures. However, hints of medieval building tradition abound in Azeroth, such as the halls at Wintergarde where the external supports mimic those found in the reconstructions of the Anglo-Saxon buildings at Cowdery's Down, Hampshire, and Yeavering, Northumberland.[54] As I previously noted, the lore of *World of Warcraft* pays particular reference to Norse myth and history, and this particular cultural reference is supported the material culture of the Viking-like Fjord settlement of Valgarde in the east of Northrend. It is highly plausible that the name is based on the famous excavations at Valsgärde, a high-status

---

52. Castles are regularly raided by enemy factions (players) as well as being the setting for the aforementioned "historical shifts."

53. For example, Wintergarde castle represents one of the main Alliance bases against King Arthas in Northrend.

54. See Martin Welch, *Anglo-Saxon England* (London: Batsford, 1992), 51-2 and color pl.1.

Viking burial site.⁵⁵ However, the buildings themselves are likely to have derived from the excavations of the Viking settlement at Hedeby, now in Germany. In particular, the timber buildings of Northrend's Valgarde with their carved dragon-headed gables and external trusses bear a marked similarity to the Viking houses reconstructed by the Haithabu Museum (Fig. 7).⁵⁶

In other instances, the influence of medievalism is less obvious. The Night Elves have an ideology that hints at older esoteric traditions. Here much attention is paid to natural places as religious sites, including reverence for ancient burial sites, such as the Dor'Danil barrow cemetery in Ashenvale. Once again comparison exists within the fragmentary evidence for the medieval pagan practices of medieval Europe. In England, evidence exists for the use/reuse of barrow sites as ritual centers at Asthall, Oxfordshire, and Sutton Hoo, Suffolk, in particular. Historical and archaeological evidence for worship in pagan Anglo-Saxon England between ca. 400 and 600 AD also includes the use of open enclosures and groves and the possible use of wooden totem poles or beams as suggested for the high status sites of Yeavering, Northumbria, and Cowdery's Down, Hampshire.⁵⁷ In Azeroth carved totems can be seen at many Night Elves' sites in Kalimdor as well as within the shamanic horde races of Orc and Tauren whose skills are based on the use of totems and relics and bear close resemblance to those of the nomadic peoples of the so-called Age of Migration in Europe (400-600AD). The early medieval period also witnessed the reuse of earlier burial monuments for secondary burial, both in barrows and close to henges.⁵⁸ At Yeavering a series of possibly Anglian pagan burials centered on a former henge prehistoric monument.⁵⁹

55. John Ljungkvist, "Valsgärde, Development and Change of a Burial Ground over 1300 years," in Svante Norr, ed., *Valsgärde Studies: the Place and its People, Past and Present.* (Uppsala: University of Uppsala, 2008), 13-55.

56. http://www.schloss-gottorf.de/wmh/index.php. Accessed 1st July 2010. However some better pictures can be viewed at www.euro-t-guide.com/See_Coun/Germany/D_NW/D_See_Viking_Museum_Haithabu_1-1.htm. Accessed 1 July 2010.

57. John Blair, "Anglo-Saxon Pagan Shrines and their Prototypes," *Anglo-Saxon Studies in Archaeology and History 8* (1995), 1-28.

58. Steve Driscoll "Picts and Prehistory: Cultural Resource Management in Early Medieval Scotland," World *Archaeology 30:1* (1998), pages 142-58, 148-9.

59. Blair, "Anglo-Saxon Pagan Shrines and their Prototypes." Some have argued for an earlier date for this burials, e.g., Sam Lucy "Early Medieval Burial at Yeavering: A Retrospective" in Paul Frodsham and Colm O'Brien, eds., *Yeavering: People, Power and*

At Milfield, Northumberland, two prehistoric henges had likewise been reused during the period.[60] In Azeroth burial mounds focussed on standing stones can be found both in Night Elves contexts in Wintergrasp, Northrend and Ashenvale, Kalimdor. It is unlikely that the examples used in *World of Warcraft* are drawn directly from the aforementioned medieval sites; nonetheless, they clearly draw from generic pagan ideas that concern nature and due reverence for ancient monuments and which have clear medieval precedent.

The Place of *World of Warcraft* in Medievalist Studies

Despite being works of high fantasy, games like *World of Warcraft* and their inherent content and environments draw indiscriminately from the medieval period, and thus are works of both popular culture and of medievalism. In the case of *World of Warcraft* the medieval is experienced both directly, through transcribed myths and "archaeological" structures, and generically, utilising, synthesising, and adapting more general materials drawn from a broad school. The medieval has long been intertwined with fantasy, particularly in the context of fantasy writing. In a digital world, this material thus provides a grounding of the familiar in a coherent and recognizable structure or framework. The balance of generic and direct influences provides a world that is instantly identifiable as loosely medievalist and yet provides enough creative context in which the game can develop unfettered by historical realism. Valgarde, for example, is recognizably and generically Viking, and the details of its buildings and architecture are drawn from archaeological example. As such they provide a framework within which a fantasy story and complex gameplay emerge. Significantly, unlike most medievalist media, such as books and film, the *World of Warcraft* is a world also subject to historical shifts providing fluidity and reinvention.[61] Thus the feel of a world in transition, and of a history that is neither static or granted, is presented to the game players. Furthermore, many such players, often from a range of backgrounds, are

---

Place (Stroud: Tempus, 2005), 127-45.

60. Lucy, "Early Medieval Burial at Yeavering," 137.

61. For example, the most recent apocalyptic Cataclysm expansion has dramatically changed some aspects of Azeroth's environment and climate and left many former buildings and temples ruinous, whilst new areas and lands have also been revealed.

consequently influenced by a range of medievalist ideas and references. That has led one commentator to go so far as to argue that studies of medievalism in popular culture can accordingly "better prepare medievalists to teach their subject" in so much that it offers a view of the Middle Ages from "the students' perspective."[62] Like it or not, computer games are now a significant part of popular culture. Future developments in game design and graphics will undoubtedly mean that medieval themes will be experienced more vividly as an alternate and fantastical medievalist world is presented and in turn experienced. In terms of popular culture, the continuing popularity of *World of Warcraft* and similar related games presents an increased and widespread active access to medievalist themes, and they are likely to continue to offer a productive area of research for medievalist studies for years to come.

---

62. David W. Marshall, "Introduction: The Medievalism of Popular Culture" in Marshall, ed., *Mass Market Medieval*, 1-13.

Arthur, Beowulf, Robin Hood, and Hollywood's Desire for Origins

William Hodapp, College of St. Scholastica

MEDIEVAL SUBJECTS HAVE CAPTURED the interest of film makers and their audiences since the advent of motion pictures in the late nineteenth century. The earliest known film on a medieval subject, Georges Méliès' *Jeanne d'Arc*, came out in 1897—less than two years after Auguste and Louis Lumière offered the first public screening of motion pictures on December 28, 1895.[1] This close connection from the medium's infancy between film and medieval subjects provokes a range of considerations for those who study and enjoy both film and medieval culture. It also underscores what's become a truism among medievalists as summed up in Umberto Eco's oft-quoted observation, "It seems that people like the Middle Ages."[2] At first blush, though, this interest in the medieval seems a bit odd. From its inception in the Renaissance, the notion of the Middle Ages—*medium aevum*—has been fundamentally one of difference, what Hans Robert Jauss calls its *Alterity*, or surprising otherness.[3] By definition, the medieval is fundamentally different from the contemporary or the modern—even though the term *modernus* was an invention of twelfth-century thinkers and writers used to distinguish themselves from

---

1. Kevin Harty, *The Reel Middle Ages: American, Western and Eastern European, Middle Eastern and Asian Films about Medieval Europe* (Jefferson, NC: McFarland, 1999), 4, 139.

2. Umberto Eco, "Dreaming of the Middle Ages," *Travels in Hyperreality: Essays* (San Diego: Harcourt, 1984), 61; qtd. in Harty, *The Reel Middle Ages*, 3, 8, and in Nickolas Haydock, *Movie Medievalism: The Imaginary Middle Ages* (Jefferson, NC: McFarland, 2008), 1, among others.

3. Hans Robert Jauss, "The Alterity and Modernity of Medieval Literature," *New Literary History* 10 (1979), 181–227.

the *antiqui*, or ancients.⁴ Used popularly today as an adjective to describe a range of social phenomena from third-world sanitary conditions to repressive, totalitarian regimes, *medieval* often connotes "backward," "nasty," "grim," and "repressive" in our daily discourse. Given the term's general status as a negative signifier, it's a wonder we remain interested in the medieval past, yet audiences do, and cinematic medievalism is a marker of that interest.

Considering this ongoing engagement with cinematic treatments of medieval subjects, I'd revise Eco's statement slightly: "It seems that people like the Middle Ages [especially as depicted in film]." And no wonder: once one has seen it, who can forget Errol Flynn in tights leading a band of merry men through the greenwood, or Robert Wagner in a page-boy wig "challenging the might of a kingdom for the kiss of a beautiful lady," or even Mel Gibson in kilt and blue face crying "Freedom" in a proto-democratic rebellion against royal tyranny?⁵ Cinematic medievalism, or "Movie Medievalism" as Nickolas Haydock calls it, is as engaging as it can be entertaining. As medievalism, it articulates a view of the Middle Ages that provides, consciously or not, a commentary or reflection on the present; as movie, it does so by means of arguably the most popular, dynamic, and commercial art form of the past 115 years. And, as in any other film category, movie medievalism also reveals film makers' preoccupations. In this essay, I explore recent instances of movie medievalism through four films: Antoine Fuqua's *King Arthur* (2004), Sturla Gunnarsson's *Beowulf and Grendel* (2005), Robert Zemeckis' *Beowulf* (2007), and Ridley Scott's *Robin Hood* (2010).⁶ Since first watching Fuqua's film in a theater in 2004, I've noticed a wish on the part of some film makers to peel back layers of legend or history to reveal the story behind the story—the "true" story. This move—what I've come to think of as a creative fulfillment of a desire for origins—points to each film maker's sense of audience as much as it does to his respective sense of history and legend, fact and fiction. In

---

4. Ernst Robert Curtius, *European Literature and the Latin Middle Ages*, trans. Willard R. Trask, *Bollingen Series 36* (Princeton: Princeton UP, 1953, 1983), 251–5.

5. *The Adventures of Robin Hood*, Dir. Michael Curtiz (Warner, 1938); *Prince Valiant*. Dir. Henry Hathaway (Twentieth Century Fox, 1954); *Braveheart*. Dir. Mel Gibson (Icon, 1995).

6. *King Arthur*, Dir. Antoine Fuqua (Touchstone, 2004); *Beowulf and Grendel*, Dir. Sturla Gunnarsson (Equinoxe, 2005); *Beowulf*, Dir. Robert Zemeckis (Paramount, 2007); *Robin Hood*, Dir. Ridley Scott (Universal, 2010).

this move, these twenty-first century film makers are not that different from nineteenth- and early twentieth-century scholars and artists, motivated by nationalistic concerns, who likewise sought true stories behind legends to fulfill an audience's wishes as well as their own.

Before examining the four films, however, I'd like to review briefly the current state of movie medievalism, or rather, the study of movie medievalism. The study of films that take medieval subjects for their plots is a relatively recent phenomenon largely conducted by people trained in medieval studies, equipped with knowledge of old languages, interested in early poetics, and skilled in a range of not-so-every-day disciplines like paleography, codicology, and iconography. (This latter discipline—iconography, or the study and interpretation of images—may explain the interest many medievalists have in film.) With this set of interests and training in the medievalist's tool kit, so to speak, it is perhaps not surprising that much study of movie medievalism centers on questions of historical accuracy: the distinction between the "reel" Middle Ages, that is, what's depicted in film on the one hand, and the "real" Middle Ages, or what is known about early cultures via investigative research on the other. For instance, in his seminal and indispensable book *The Reel Middle Ages*, published in 1999, Kevin Harty surveys movie medievalism and catalogs nearly six hundred films made from 1897 through 1996, thereby establishing a seedbed for further work. Taking up the reel/real distinction Harty suggests in a number of his entries, John Aberth, in his 2003 study *A Knight at the Movies: Medieval History on Film*, advances this approach by comparing what is known of medieval subjects, say of Arthur or Norse culture, to how they're depicted in film, usually to the latter's detriment.[7]

Scholars have recently critiqued this fidelity model of criticism largely on the grounds that it ignores the film as film, with its own contingency, technique, genre, and approach to history.[8] In his 2008 book *Movie Medievalism: The Imaginary Middle Ages*, Nickolas Haydock argues for a re-examination of the "reel/real" dichotomy, asking simply two related questions: "Are the reel Middle Ages to be defined and studied chiefly in terms of error? And where exactly are to be found the real Middle Ages

---

7. *A Knight at the Movies: Medieval History on Film* (New York: Routledge, 2003).

8. Richard Burt, "Getting Schmedieval: Of Manuscript and Film Prologues, Paratexts, and Parodies," *Exemplaria* 19 (2007), 217-8; see also Laurie A. Finke and Martin B. Schichtman, *Cinematic Illuminations: The Middle Ages on Film* (Baltimore: Johns Hopkins UP, 2009), 53-67.

that this terminology presupposes?"⁹ Drawing on Jacques Lacan's ideas of the imaginary and the real to begin an answer to his own questions, Haydock posits a relationship between "screen dreams and daydreams" where both are a form of reverie in relation to the real. He continues:

> With historical films this production of reverie is considerably more powerful [than with non-historical films] because the "reality-effects" of film are not immediately contravened by the reality principle. That is to say, ideas formed during a film set in contemporary times may linger beyond the cinema experience, but soon give way to more mundane experiences that are not packed with heroic action, beautiful people, or poetically just consequences. Our ideas about the distant past are perhaps more vulnerable to the lure of the cinema because there is no immediate access to falsification. The very alterity of the Middle Ages works to make it an especially potent preserve of fantasy, the realm par excellence of the Imaginery. . . . [T]here are very few people indeed who do not imagine Arthur fighting on horseback in plate armor, Joan of Arc as a battle-hardened proto-feminist, or William Wallace as a short, tartan-clad peasant.¹⁰

With movie medievalism, then, we find a strange movement back and forth between the alterity, or surprising otherness, of a distant past and its reconstruction in film makers and their audiences' immediate present: a reconstruction made possible only by implementing quite nonmedieval technologies in curiously enough a work setting most medieval artisans would find familiar—a collective enterprise advancing an artistic project. For film makers and the many artisans involved, the collective enterprise results in a film that, like a medieval cathedral in its visual art and liturgy, seeks to recover a past through storytelling.

1. The Coming of the King: Antoine Fuqua's King Arthur

Arguably movie medievalism's most productive source of grist for the cinematic mill centers on stories of Arthur and his knights. Since Edwin S. Porter's 1904 film of Richard Wagner's *Parsifal*, the earliest known Arthurian film, film makers have made some one hundred Arthurian

---

9. *Movie Medievalism*, 6.
10. *Movie Medievalism*, 11.

movies.[11] One of the more recent is Antoine Fuqua's *King Arthur*, released in theaters in July 2004, coincidentally a hundred years after Porter's premiere of *Parsifal*—a detail suggesting a rough average of one Arthurian film annually during the period separating these two films. Briefly, *King Arthur* takes place at the end of Roman occupation of Britain, one would think about 407/10 CE when the last known Roman legion stationed in Britannia withdrew though the date projected early in the film is "452 AD" [sic], which with an additional text scroll "15 Years Later" sets the story in 467 CE. The film centers on one Artorius Castus, a Romano-Celtic leader of a small contingent of Sarmatian knights forced into the service of the Roman Empire. These knights bear names from medieval Arthurian romances—Lancelot, Bors, Dagonet, Tristram, Gawain, and Galahad—and with Arthur they have just completed a fifteen-year tour of duty fighting Woads, as the Picts are called in the film. Instead of discharging them as expected, an Imperial delegate from Rome named Bishop Germanus orders Arthur and his knights on a final mission to rescue a Roman Senator named Marius and his family from certain death at the hands of invading Saxons. Senator Marius lives in Pictish territory three days' ride north of Hadrian's Wall. Reluctantly, Arthur leads his men on what all consider a suicide mission, freeing a number of enslaved Woads from Marius while being chased by a numerically superior company of Saxon warriors. Ingeniously, in a rearguard action on a frozen lake, Arthur and company manage to drown the Saxons by causing them to break through the ice while Marius' family and the group of Woads head for the Wall. One of the rescued Woads, as it happens, turns out to be Guinevere, who not only fights alongside Arthur and his knights but also later convinces Arthur to remain in Britain. Though successful, the mission is not without loss as Dagonet dies in the fight on the ice. The Saxons reach the wall not long after Arthur, and the next day, as the dust of the Roman retreat settles, Arthur and his former-enemies-turned-allies, the Woads, prepare for battle. The remaining Sarmatians—now free with their discharge scrolls in hand—initially leave with the retreating Roman unit only to come to Arthur's aid as their horses sense an impending fight. In the film's final battle, Tristram and Lancelot die, but Arthur, Guinevere, and company succeed in defeating the Saxon hoard. The film's action closes with mar-

---

11. Kevin Harty, "Arthurian Film," *An Arthuriana/Camelot Project Bibliography* (Rochester: Camelot Project, 1997). Accessed 16 November 2010.

riage between Arthur and Guinevere, Merlin declaring Arthur king, and Arthur declaring "Let every man, woman, and child bear witness that from this day all Britons will be united in one common cause."

Other scholars have taken the film to task for its fidelity, and I'll not rehearse at length here its several improbabilities: for instance, the incongruity of the date of its setting as coinciding with the departure of the Romans from Britain, nor the inexplicable presence of an obviously successful Roman villa in the midst of hostile territory a full three-day ride from security, nor the advance of a Saxon army from the north, nor the overly simplistic ethnic characterization of Romans and Saxons as bad, Sarmatians and Woads as good, nor even the Sarmatian theory itself. Tom Shippey and others have addressed many of these points already.[12] What I am curious about, though, is the film makers' sense of what they thought they were doing. Trained in paleography and codicology, and reminded by Richard Burt to pay attention to prologues and cinematic paratexts, that is, "opening title sequences, trailers, movie posters; interviews with film makers and historian consultants. . . DVD audiocommentaries. . . deleted scenes, animated menus, official film websites" et cetera,[13] I can't help but approach film much as I would a medieval manuscript. For, just as early texts written in manuscripts are frequently mediated through paratexts like commentaries, glosses, prologues, illuminations, rubrics, and initials, twenty-first century films are becoming ever more mediated as well. If for instance we look at the film's poster, an image of which is available online,[14] we can guess a fair amount about what the film's makers and marketers want us think. Looking at the poster's image and first bit of text, which reads in white letters "From The Producers Of 'The Pirates of the Caribbean,'" I'd say we're in for a swashbuckling, swords-and-arrows, proto-feminist-warrior adventure; looking at the rubrics—the red-lettered text (a medieval convention)—we're also in for an Arthur-Guinevere-Lancelot relational triangle while a disembodied but silent voice commands *Rule Your Destiny July 7*; finally, and perhaps most importantly we're given in another set of white letters below the

---

12. Tom Shippey, "Fuqua's *King Arthur*: More Myth-making in America," *Exemplaria* 19 (2007), 312–3.

13. Burt, "Getting Schmedieval," 218.

14. An image of the *King Arthur* movie poster is available at http://www.melwesson.com/images/posters-large/kingarthur.jpg (accessed March 14, 2011).

film's title what seems to be its subtitle, "The Untold True Story that Inspired the Legend."

Turning to the film itself, we're oriented immediately by a textual prologue that assumes a literate audience: one that not only can read but also knows something about the medieval Arthur, though not too much. The unattributed text—another disembodied, silent voice—states quite confidently: "Historians agree that the classical 15th century tale of King Arthur and his Knights rose from a real hero who lived a thousand years earlier in a period often called the Dark Ages. Recently discovered archeological evidence sheds new light on his true identity." This prologue—though inaccurate in detail—effectively constructs and orients its audience to the film's point of view, thereby mediating its viewing. Setting up a single "classical 15th century tale" as a straw man against which the film is positioned (is the prologue perhaps referring to Sir Thomas Malory's collection of Arthurian stories?), the text constructs an audience interested in "real" heroes, familiar with the phrase "the Dark Ages," impressed by results of scientific discovery, and curious about Arthur's "true identity." I remember feeling a mix of amusement and alienation on first reading this prologue in the theater: I wasn't part of the audience for whom the text was constructed, since I knew things weren't as straightforward and clear as the prologue declares. Arthurian literature is diverse and messy and Arthurian history scant.

Following the prologue, Fuqua frames the film with an image of a modern map and a series of brief scenes interlaced with a narrator's voice, who we quickly learn is Lancelot. Lancelot introduces what passes in the film for the Sarmatian experience with Rome and narrates his personal experience in order to orient and draw the audience further into the story. He says:

> By 300 AD [sic] the Roman Empire extended from Arabia to Britain. But they wanted more: more land, more peoples loyal and subservient to Rome, but no people so important as the powerful Sarmatians to the East. Thousands died on that field. And when the smoke cleared on the fourth day, the only Sarmatian soldiers left alive were members of the decimated but legendary cavalry. The Romans, impressed by their bravery and horsemanship, spared their lives. In exchange, these warriors were incorporated into the Roman military—better they had died that day. For the second part of the bargain they had struck indebted not only themselves

Arthur, Beowulf, Robin Hood, and Hollywood's Desire for Origins

but also their sons, and their sons, and so on, to serve the Empire as knights. I was such a son... Our post was Britain, or at least the Southern half. For the land was divided by a seventy-three-mile wall built three centuries before us to protect the Empire from the native fighters from the North. So, as our forefathers had done, we made our way and reported to our commander in Britain, ancestrally named for the first Artorius, or Arthur.

Like an introductory chapter to a book, Lancelot's narrative moves us to the story's present moment in 467 CE, which gets underway almost immediately with a fight in which our seven heroes come to the rescue of a carriage under attack by Woads: whether intentional or not, this episode echoes Kurosawa's *Seven Samurai* (1954), Sturges' *The Magnificent Seven* (1960), Zucker's *First Knight* (1995), and Hollywood Westerns in which the cavalry ride in at the last moment. This episode also reinforces Lancelot's history lesson: these Sarmatians are tough fighters, the Woads know it, and the Romans guarding the carriage—as well as the audience watching the film—soon learn it. And their main preoccupation besides fighting is freedom. Shippey argues convincingly that—though the film explores ethnicity and race—freedom, in fact, is its theme[15]: freedom from Rome; freedom from Saxon terror; freedom from slavery, torture, and an oppressive Christianity; freedom to choose one's destiny—just as the film poster declares. In this last idea the film is as much a *bildungsroman* as it is adventure tale, and its optimistic ending, with marriage and coronation of sorts rolled into one, suggests a new beginning that belies what historians actually do know about late fifth-century Britain. Arthur, if there really was an Arthur, may have won the battle, but the Britons lost the war.

Shippey sums his brief critique of the film's fidelity to history, saying "perhaps the least truthful part about the Fuqua film comes in the first two words of the opening credits, 'Historians agree. . .' On this subject, historians do not agree about anything."[16] Fuqua himself seems a bit unsure, or perhaps shy, of the film's truth claims. In the audio commentary accompanying the director's cut DVD, an authorial interpretive layer in which he tries to mediate a reading of the film, Fuqua says:

---

15. Shippey, "Fuqua's *King Arthur*," 314–6.
16. Shippey, "Fuqua's *King Arthur*," 313.

> People talk about whether King Arthur existed or didn't exist, and nobody really knows. But we do know there was a battle at Badon Hill, and there was a man there by the name of Artorius Castus who defeated the Saxons. And I figured if you're going to make a film about King Arthur why not try to find some sort of reality to it. . . . [I]t's basically the prequel as far as I'm concerned: before the magical legends and stories took over.

As Fuqua declares quite openly here about Arthur's existence, "nobody really knows"; what he lists as fact—the battle at "Badon Hill" and "Artorius Castus"—however, are also open to question, for neither exists in any account contemporaneous with the time of the supposed event. More importantly, Fuqua suggests, perhaps unknowingly, that the act of making the film was in a real sense an act of wish fulfillment: an attempt "to find some sort of reality," a "prequel. . . before the magical legends and stories took over." Yet, as anyone who digs into to the subject learns fairly quickly, historical records say little, and archeological evidence remains inconclusive. At film's end, Lancelot—the dead, would-be lover of Guinevere—gets the last say in a final, framing voice over that's part foreshadowing, part unconscious acknowledgement of the fictive nature of the whole enterprise: "And as for the knights who gave their lives, their deaths were cause for neither mourning nor sadness. For they will live forever in the names and deeds handed down from father to son, mother to daughter in the legends of King Arthur and his knights."

2. Translating Narrative to Screen: Sturla Gunnarsson's Beowulf and Grendel and Robert Zemekis' Beowulf

Compared to Arthurian literature, with its linguistic and generic variety, the Old English narrative poem *Beowulf* seems rather stable in spite of the fact that many things about it remain unsettled: its date, for instance, its place of origin, or even its textual status. That the poem is *the* single instance of a long, heroic Old English narrative surviving from Anglo-Saxon culture assures its place in literary histories; that it also tells a compelling story, layered in with other stories, is a bonus; that it even survives at all in a single, fire-damaged manuscript copy is just short of a miracle. The main action of the story separates into two sections of uneven length. In the first, Beowulf is a young Geatish hero who comes to the aid of Hrothgar and his Danes, embattled by Grendel, an elusive, violent "moor-stalker," and his mother. Defeating both, Beowulf returns home and, in the poem's second section, eventually becomes king of the Geats. After fifty years on the throne, he dies fighting a ravaging dragon, which he slays with help from Wiglaf, a young retainer. Unlike Arthur stories, and in spite of its relative stability as a text, *Beowulf* garnered no attention from film makers until 1999 when Graham Baker loosely adapted the poem in his science-fiction film *Beowulf*.[17] Coincidentally in the same year John McTiernan, with *The 13th Warrior*, offered a film version of Michael Crichton's novel *Eaters of the Dead*, which Crichton based on *Beowulf* and on Ahmad Ibn-Fadlan's tenth-century ethnographic account of Norsemen.[18] This lack of attention may not surprise: though an engaging heroic narrative, the poem offers little in the way of visual description: we never know specifics about the hero's appearance, nor do we have a clear idea of what Grendel, his Dam, or the Dragon look like. Heorot—the target of Grendel's attacks—is a mead hall with a door and beams, but that's about all the poem offers. And descriptions of neither landscape nor seascape figure much into the story. For the *Beowulf* poet and his audience, it would seem, physical description was much less important than characterization and motivation as revealed through speech, action, and the act of storytelling itself. Sturla Gunnarsson in 2005 and Robert Zemeckis in 2007 both addressed this lack of cinematic attention as each translated the Old English narrative poem into twenty-first century film.[19]

Any given text—whether Old English poem or twenty-first century film—is an artifact of its culture as well as the product of an author, director, poet, playwright. Translation involves, quite literally, the "carrying over" of such a text from its originating cultural group to another culturally different group so that an audience in the second group might access the text. André Lefevere calls this second group a "target culture" and argues a translator must carefully attend to both target-culture needs and the original text's "universe of discourse," or those elements implicit and explicit in the text that point to its originating culture.[20] In medieval

---

17. *Beowulf*, Dir. Graham Baker (Capitol Films, 1999).

18. Michael Crichton, *Eaters of the Dead: The Manuscript of Ibn Fadlan, Relating His Experiences with the Northmen in A.D. 922* (New York: Knopf, 1976); *The 13th Warrior*, Dir. John McTiernan (Touchstone, 1999).

19. *Beowulf and Grendel*, Dir. Sturla Gunnarsson; *Beowulf*, Dir. Robert Zemeckis.

20. André Lefevere, *Translating Literature: Practice and Theory in a Comparative Literature Context* (New York: MLA, 1992), 86, 120.

theory, the notion of "translatio" encompassed texts rendered both literally and freely, and from one medium or genre to another.[21] Thus, both a play such as the York Crucifixion and a wood carving such as the Gero Crucifix translate the Gospel narratives of Jesus' death into active dramatic representation on the one hand and static visual representation on the other. Such a second text produced through an act of translation offers a reading, or interpretation, of the original text: a point Douglas Kelly emphasizes in his discussion of medieval "interpretatio."[22] Frequently, this second text serves not as surrogate but more so as replacement for the original. As I argue elsewhere, *Beowulf* itself seems to be a translation of earlier oral and perhaps written texts, and so it has invited scholarly scrutiny regarding sources and analogues.[23] In the nineteenth and early twentieth centuries, for instance, scholars worked the poem as though it were an archaeological site, digging and sifting in search of an original story lying beneath layers of Christian Anglo-Saxon cultural debris. This search for origins underlay particularly the nineteenth-century *Liedertheorie*, which assumed that several poets composed the poem over time by interpolating folk tales and myths: the scholar's task, then, was to discover those original sources somehow in the text.[24] Though this approach yielded little, we can see from the poem itself why scholars initially thought it might be fruitful, for the poet in several places emphasizes differences between his own target culture—a Christian Anglo-Saxon culture shared with his audience—and the universe of discourse which the world of the

21. For translation theory in medieval culture, see Jeanette Beer, "Introduction," *Medieval Translators and their Craft*, ed. Jeanette Beer, *Studies in Medieval Culture 25* (Kalamazoo, MI: Medieval Institute, 1989), 1–7, and Rita Copeland, *Rhetoric, Hermeneutics, and Translation in the Middle Ages: Academic Traditions and Vernacular Texts*, Cambridge Studies in Medieval Literature 11 (Cambridge: Cambridge UP, 1991), 9–62 and 151–78.

22. Douglas Kelly, "The *Fidus interpres*: Aid or Impediment to Medieval Translation and Translatio?" *Translation Theory and Practice in the Middle Ages*, ed. Jeanette Beer, *Studies in Medieval Culture* 38 (Kalamazoo, MI: Medieval Institute, 1997), 47–8.

23. William F. Hodapp, "'No hie fæder cunnon': But Twenty-First Century Film Makers Do," *Essays in Medieval Studies* 26 (2010), 102–3.

24. Ernst Moritz Ludwig Ettmüller first advanced this theory in 1840, and it came to dominate much discussion for the remainder of the nineteenth century, especially among German-speaking scholars. See Friedrich Klaeber, ed., *Beowulf and the Fight at Finnsburg*, 3rd ed. (Lexington, 1959), cii–ciii, and T.A. Shippey and Andreas Haarder, eds., *Beowulf: The Critical Heritage* (London, 1998), 28–74, which also includes translations of Ettmüller and others.

story itself evokes: a Geatish-Danish world of a distant past with its own values and assumptions. Just as it seems to have drawn on source texts, elusive though they are, *Beowulf* has inspired in its own right a variety of translations from modern English prose and verse renderings to renderings in different media such as film.

In *Beowulf and Grendel*, Sturla Gunnarsson translates the first part of the poem—the fights with Grendel and his mother—from narrative to cinematic drama. Starting again with one of the film's paratexts, the movie poster,[25] we're oriented immediately to the chief preoccupation of the film's makers and marketers. Reading the poster from back to front, we notice first a background image of a manuscript folio with faded lettering over which are layered three more images: on the upper left appears a turned-profile man in chainmail looking past the viewer's right and on the middle right a square-sailed long ship floating on water; at the bottom we see a troop of some fifteen mounted men galloping. Names of four chief actors and the film's title separate the upper two-thirds from the bottom third while the text "*Beneath the Legend Lies the Tale*" is superimposed in the upper right, above the ship and layered over the manuscript image. Those familiar with folio 129r from British Library MS. Cotton Vitellius A.XV would on close inspection recognize the poster's background manuscript image as the first page of *Beowulf*. Layering other images and modern English text over the manuscript page, effectively erasing the Old English poem, reveals the kind of translation this film intends to be: a replacement text of sorts carrying over the pre-legendary tale from the sixth- to the twenty-first century. The film itself reinforces this reading of the poster.

The film opens with a continuous telescoping shot of a map of sixth-century Scandinavia. As the camera pans in on Daneland and Geatland, five lines of text appear with a voice-over recitation from someone whom we later learn is a Geatish poet-warrior named Thorkill:

> Hwaet! Great are the tales of the Spear-Danes
> How they broke and bloodied their foes
> How they tamed the Northern seas
> Some tales sail, others sink
> Below the waves but no less true. . .

---

25. An image of the *Beowulf and Grendel* movie poster is available at http://www.moviesonline.ca/movie-gallery/albums/userpics//poster_BeowulfAndGrendelPoster2.jpg (accessed March 14, 2011).

With this mix of text and oral recitation—no doubt implying the transition from an oral to a literate culture—Gunnarsson suggests the film tells a "true" story that has somehow sunk "Below the waves": again, the tale that lies beneath the legend, as the movie poster declares. Not content with the poem's explanation for Grendel's attack on Heorot, that he despised the sound of merrymaking in the mead hall, Gunnarsson adopts the language of the book and stages a sequence of scenes entitled "Prologue: A Hate is Born." In this prologue, a troll-child witnesses a gang of armed horsemen, vastly superior in number and weaponry, surprise and murder his father without evident cause: these horsemen, we later learn, are Hrothgar and his men. This apparently racially-motivated murder repeats the trope common in films from *Star Wars* (1977) and *Platoon* (1986) to *Braveheart* (1995) and *Avatar* (2009) of a dominant culture using its political power and might to control and suppress a minority culture. Spared, the child, a.k.a. Grendel, grows to adulthood, planning revenge: a plan with which the audience sympathizes to a degree. As the film presents the story's main outline—Grendel's attack, Hrothgar's inability to defend Heorot, Beowulf's arrival and eventual confrontation with Grendel, his subsequent defeat of Grendel's Dam, and his departure from Daneland—it also adds details, presumably the bits of the story that lie "below the waves but no less true," particularly a character named Selma. As a marginal figure herself in Daneland, Selma serves as conduit between Danes and Geats on one side and trolls on the other by being both mother of Grendel's son and, later and briefly, Beowulf's lover. Serving as the film's moral center by advancing an anti-racist outlook, she leads Beowulf to a deeper understanding of, even sympathy for, Grendel. Given the chance to slay Grendel's son—half human, half troll—after killing his Dam, Beowulf defers, much as Hrothgar did at film's beginning. In the film's penultimate episode, the camera observes Beowulf as he builds a rock cairn in Grendel's honor in hope of making restitution in some way for his role in Grendel's death. Having witnessed the murder of Grendel's father, as well as Grendel's demise, the film's audience—the viewer the film constructs—welcomes Beowulf's transformation in this moment.

Loaded with dramatic irony, the film undermines both Danes and Geats and their traditional means of storytelling. Taking a cue from *Beowulf* itself, which includes scenes of poetic composition and performance within the narrative, Gunnarsson shows the poet-warrior Thorkill, the voice of the film's opening narration, composing a tale based on their adventures in Daneland. Shortly after Grendel's fatal wounding, for instance, we see him telling a tale of the events to a group of children. In Thorkill's story, Beowulf heroically engages Grendel in single, hand-to-hand combat. Overhearing the tale, Beowulf breaks the narration, chases off the children, and accuses his friend of telling lies. Beowulf's response to Thorkill's narrative serves to control the audience's response as well: like Beowulf, the film's audience—having witnessed the fight in which Grendel cuts off his own arm in a desperate effort to escape—grows suspicious of the poet. Knowing the truth of Grendel's demise as delivered via the camera, the audience that the camera itself constructs rejects Thorkill's version as simply untrue. Similarly, the film concludes with yet another nod to the bard, whom we see composing more of the song and linking Grendel to Cain, the son of the biblical Adam and Eve who slew his brother Abel: again, a reference to the poem. Hearing the song, one shipmate asks for commentary from another, who explains Cain and Grendel are linked because both are killers. This reading of Thorkill's poem draws a brief "reader-response": observing they're all killers, the first Geat states dismissively, "Thorkill's song is shit." By film's end, Thorkill's voice—the voice with which the film opens in its claim that "Some tales sail, others sink / Below the waves though no less true"—is completely dismissed, replaced by the true tale lying "*Beneath the Legend*" as revealed through film.

As I've argued elsewhere, when we place Zemekis' animated *Beowulf* alongside Gunnarsson's live-action film, we note a number of similarities in detail in spite of fundamental differences in style and method.[26] For instance, both choose to stage Christians within the world of the story, a detail that's not part of the Old English narrative, and the Christians they stage—an Irish monk named Brendan in Gunnarsson's film and Unferth himself in Zemekis'—come across as mad in the one case and brutal and cowardly in the other. They also both depict Hrothgar as near naked and drunk early in the film, thereby suggesting ineffectual leadership at best from the beginning. These and other details, such as the way Beowulf traps Grendel by securing his arm with a chain rather than by his hand grip as the poem has it, suggest Zemeckis knows Gunnarsson's film well. Zemeckis, however, delivers a version of the story that is nearly polar opposite to Gunnarsson. Viewing the movie's posters for starters, his version

---

26. Hodapp, "'No hie fæder cunnon,'" 104.

of *Beowulf* seems clearly a morality tale rather than *bildungsroman* as in Gunnarsson's film. In one poster, an image of which is available online,[27] an animated, sharply-focused image of a man's face, shoulder, and right arm dominate the upper half of the page. Staring directly into the viewers' eyes, he holds a sword in his right hand, thrusting it toward the viewer so the point—fading out of focus—gives the impression of being just inches away and nearly breaking through the image itself. Text overlays the image in the bottom quarter: a list of five actors' names, followed by the film's title, credits, and release information. The only other text is a phrase imposed in the middle right, stating "*Pride is the Curse.*" The text's placement suggests that the man—Beowulf himself, we later discover—is making this statement while pointing directly at the viewer with his sword. Though seemingly addressed to the viewer, the statement refers primarily to Beowulf, as the film bears out, yet it also re-enforces the film's morality tale quality: it serves as both an introduction to a key theme and a warning to the audience about the dangers of pride. With this emphasis on morality, Zemeckis' treatment of the theme of storytelling is significantly different from Gunnarsson's.

Unlike Gunnarsson, who states outright that the story's chief liar is the poet, Zemeckis—through his use of a never-lying camera's gaze—undercuts Beowulf himself as he spins tales that don't match what the audience sees. In the flyting scene with Unferth, for instance, a key moment early in poem and film alike, Beowulf responds to Unferth's challenge regarding his swimming contest with Breca, another hero, by spinning a tale that portrays himself in a good light in spite of his loss of the race. As he tells of being attacked by sea creatures, the camera and its audience witness the fight as though they had been present. Near tale's end, Beowulf claims having slain all the sea creatures, but the camera witnesses him being seduced by a mermaid instead. Beowulf's words don't match his deeds as the camera reveals the events, and the audience constructed by the film unquestioningly accepts the camera's point of view as a reliable record.

Zemeckis plays with this ironic point of view elsewhere in the film, but perhaps the most important series of scenes that undercut the hero is his confrontation with Grendel's Dam in a water cave. As depicted, this scene becomes the central conflict of this version of the story rather than

---

27. An image of the *King Arthur* movie poster is available at http://www.melwesson.com/images/posters-large/kingarthur.jpg (accessed March 14, 2011).

the sidebar fight it seems to be in both the poem and Gunnarsson's film. After observing the hero swim to a water cave, the camera closely watches Beowulf engage Grendel's mother: a beautiful water-demon. During their exchange, Grendel's Dam seduces Beowulf, promising him power, wealth, and a long life. In the wake of the earlier stories of Beowulf's swimming contest with Breca, in which the camera's visual narrative overwhelms Beowulf's verbal narrative, the film's audience isn't surprised by the hero's weakness in this episode: he seems particularly vulnerable to sexual temptation. Upon returning to Heorot, Beowulf tries to cover up his folly by claiming he killed the "hag" in a fight, which he describes much as the narrator tells it in the poem. Hrothgar, who we later discover is Grendel's father, questions Beowulf's story in private, saying "she's no hag, Beowulf; we both know that: but answer me, did you kill her?" Beowulf's response—"Would I have been able to escape her had I not?"—is disingenuous at best, for Hrothgar and the film's audience both know the answer is yes. When the film's audience realizes later that Beowulf's union with Grendel's Dam results in the Dragon—his own son whom he fights and kills in the film's final battle scene—Zemeckis' morality tale comes full circle: Beowulf is the source of his own downfall and the demise of many others. As Zemeckis translates the Old English poem into film, he uses the old text as platform to explore ironically the modern hero: the threat to the community present in Grendel and the Dragon is primarily the result not of external forces at work, but of Hrothgar's and Beowulf's internal weaknesses.

Gunnarsson and Zemeckis might be surprised, I think, to learn they have solved a conundrum through the imaginary art of film: they provide the elusive source for the Old English poem sought after for so long by so many nineteenth- and early twentieth-century scholars—at least that's the implication of their truth claims. In their desire for origins, for the "true" tale that has sunk "beneath the waves," each film maker takes a different tack in translating the poem to film, but the general result is the same. Gunnarsson's *Beowulf and Grendel* emphasizes Beowulf's development as a character from reactive-warrior seeking battle to thoughtful-warrior seeking understanding. Because the film's prologue sensitizes viewers to the injustice of the Danes, the audience the film constructs desires this growth in Beowulf. Zemeckis' *Beowulf*, on the other hand, emphasizes the hero's corruption, thereby distancing the audience from him. This Beowulf fails and like many a modern-day political leader succumbs to

A Year's Work in Midievalism

temptations of sex, power, wealth, and longevity. As Robert Zemeckis states in a documentary about making the film, "This has nothing to do with the *Beowulf* you were forced to read in junior high school: it's all about eating, drinking, killing, and fornicating."[28] And, one might add, it's about the curse of pride, just as the movie poster states. Both Beowulfs are twenty-first century men: as Gunnarsson's Beowulf grows in sensitivity and openness to difference, Zemeckis' becomes more and more corrupt. In neither cinematic translation of *Beowulf*, however, is the traditional mode of story-telling, so strongly evident in the poem, considered reliable. Rather, the camera's eye replaces the narrator's voice and undercuts the story-tellers dramatized in each film. In their desire for origins, both film makers imagine themselves, or rather they reveal their perceptions of early twenty-first century culture, as they translate the Old English poem to film. Participating fully in the target culture the film makers assume, the audiences these films construct—as with the audience presupposed by Fuqua's *King Arthur*—elide the essentially fictional nature of film and see the imagined origin, the tale beneath the legend, as somehow truer than anything a lying poet or story-telling hero could create.

3. The Making of an Outlaw: Ridley Scott's Robin Hood

I remember distinctly first viewing the trailer for Ridley Scott's *Robin Hood*, what's labeled "Trailer #1" in the bonus tracks of the director's cut DVD. Having been thinking for some time about the issue of Hollywood's medieval imaginary, particularly the effort of some film makers to fulfill a desire for origins, I was immediately taken by the trailer's premise. Its series of action images—underpinned initially by natural sounds that morph into a hard rock pulse—serve as the setting for its textual message, which appears interspersed among the images as six unvoiced passages in white text on black backdrop: "*From Ridley Scott Director of 'Gladiator'*"; "*Academy Award Winner Russel Crowe*"; "*Academy Award Winner Cate Blanchett*"; "*Universal Pictures Presents*"; "*The Story Behind the Legend*"; "*The Hero Behind the Outlaw.*" The only voiced text in the trailer, Russell Crowe saying "Rise, and Rise Again, until lambs become lions," immediately follows the sixth passage. The trailer concludes with the title "*Robin

---

28. "A Hero's Journey: The Making of *Beowulf*," Ex. Prod. Mark Herzog (Paramount, 2008).

Hood," the statement "*Coming 2010*," and brief credits. I thought, "well isn't this interesting—now a Robin Hood movie that's romancing origins." The movie's poster, again an image of which is available online,[29] bore out my initial impression of the trailer. Dominated by an image of a charging figure on horseback, war hammer in hand and screaming, the poster re-states the trailer's chief message with an overlaid text in the upper left: "*The Untold Story of the Man Behind the Legend.*" The image—obviously of Robin Hood—re-enforces the "untold" portion of the message: noticeably absent are the iconic accoutrements associated with the man in green, his bow and arrows. Rather, echoing his Maximus character in *Gladiator*, Russell Crowe appears here as a man-at-arms in full charge.

This claim for the film as depicting the Robin Hood origin story is intriguing, for like Arthurian literature the Robin Hood tradition is as messy and diverse as can be. Usually set in the late twelfth to early thirteenth century, during the reigns of Richard the Lion Heart and John Lackland, Robin Hood tales in the form of ballads, plays, and one longish narrative poem recount daring-do adventures.[30] Unlike Arthur, who represents political authority and unity, Robin Hood is an outlaw, undermining and resisting authority at every turn. In most stories, he's a just-minded outlaw, though: an affable, roguish character who famously steals from the rich to give to the poor. In many stories set in the 1190s, while Richard is away on Crusade, Robin Hood particularly stands for right in the face of Prince John's repressive regime, represented by the Sheriff of Nottingham and certain officious ecclesiasts. Occasional tales show a dark side, but for the most part Robin, Maid Marian, and the band of merry men live a life free from want, authority, and social control in Sherwood Forest, Nottinghamshire. Such are the bits that make up the legend. The promise of Scott's trailer and poster is a film that, like Fuqua's *King Arthur*, tells the story of how things got that way. Yet it's still very much a Hollywood story.

In a by now quite familiar pattern, the film opens with a textual prologue designed, much like prologues to medieval plays, to orient audience

29. An image of the *Robin Hood* movie poster I discuss here is available at http://filmviews.info/wp-content/uploads/2010/07/robin-hood-2010-20100419091140953_640w.jpg (accessed March 14, 2011).

30. See Stephen Knight and Thomas Ohlgren, eds., *Robin Hood and Other Outlaw Tales*(Kalamazoo, Michigan: Medieval Institute, 2000) for an introduction and accessible anthology of early Robin Hood texts.

members to the tale they're about to see and hear. As with *King Arthur*, this prologue is not voiced and therefore assumes a basically literate audience who can read the following: "In times of tyranny and injustice when law oppresses the people, the outlaw takes his place in history. England at the turn of the 12th century was such a time." An episode set in Nottingham and illustrating England's lawless state, in which thieves from the forest steal a manor house's seed grain, immediately follows. Another text then punctuates this episode: "King Richard the Lion Heart, bankrupt of wealth and glory, is plundering his way back to England after ten years on his Crusade. In his army is an archer named Robin Longstride. This is the story of his return home where, for defending the weak against the strong, he will be condemned to live outside the law." With the use of "plundering" to describe Richard's actions, this second text suggests England's leadership is morally as well as fiscally bankrupt. And in a nod to Kevin Reynolds' *Robin Hood: Prince of Thieves* (1991), the text also reveals the film's underlying story pattern: we have here an instance of *nostos*, a return tale.

Like Odysseus in Homer's *Odyssey*, Orfeo in the Middle English poem *Sir Orfeo*, or Robin Locksley in Reynolds' *Robin Hood* film, Longstride's return is unconventional. Arrested and placed in stocks for speaking the truth to the King, Robin and his mates Will Scarlet, Allan a' Dale, and Little John escape when Richard is killed in battle, only to thwart an ambush in which Sir Robin Locksley, Richard's aide-de-camp, is killed while carrying the crown post-haste to England. Seizing the opportunity to gain wealth, and declaring a bit boldly to Allan a' Dale's objections, Longstride says: "How do you know that the knights you see walking about are actually knights at all? There is no difference between a knight and any other man aside from what he wears. All we need is about us: armor, helmets, swords—and we make England wealthy men with horses and gold." Disguised as knights, with Longstride assuming the name Sir Robin Locksley, they arrive in England, manage to discharge their duty with the crown, and hot-foot it to Nottingham. Once there, Sir Walter Locksley encourages Longstride to continue the ruse of the son returned home from war to keep the taxman at bay. What follows is a story in which Longstride and Locksley's widow, Marian, gradually work together to restore the farmstead. Longstride learns of his father's fate—a proto-democratic organizer squashed by royal authority—and the two eventually fall in love. Meanwhile, treason is afoot as King John's trusted friend

Godfrey violently enforces repressive taxation in an effort to turn nobles against the King. Ever a weak-minded monarch, and finally informed of Godfrey's plan, John manages to meet with the nobles at Barnsdale before they openly rebel. Too old to attend the meeting himself, Sir Walter Locksley sends Longstride as his representative. It's here where the two storylines merge when Longstride, speaking for Sir Walter, argues for a charter of liberties for Englishmen. In answer to the King's quip—"So, what would you have, hmm? A castle for every man?"—Longstride replies, anachronistically of course but to great cheering from the soldiers, "every Englishman's home is his castle."[31] King John agrees to the charter, and the army advances against an immanent threat from France. With plenty of action, the film moves to its close: Godfrey murders Sir Walter, the English defeat a French invasion, King John refuses to honor his pledge for the charter of liberties, he outlaws Longstride for advocating for such a charter, and Robin and Marian and company move to the greenwood. In a voice over, Marian says: "The greenwood is the outlaw's friend. Now the orphan boys make us welcome: no tax, no tithe, nobody rich, nobody poor, fair shares for all at nature's table, many wrongs to be righted in the country of King John. Watch over us, Walter." One final text, written in the same script as the prologue, frames the film: "And so the legend begins."

Just as trailer and poster promise, we have here a movie in which film makers seek to realize their own imaginary origins of Robin Hood and of the Middle Ages. In a documentary on the making of the film,[32] Ridley Scott reveals this desire for origins when he says "I would've liked to have lived in any one of the films I've made: you've got to want to occupy that space." Echoing Scott, Brian Grazer, co-producer with Scott and Russell Crowe, states: "You know, I wanted to experience the Crusades, experience a really brutal time." The "space" and "time" Scott and Grazer desire in this case—late twelfth-century England—is an imaginary space intentionally colored by Scott's previous film collaborations with Crowe,

---

31. This phrase originates not in the twelfth century, but in 1628 in Sir Edward Coke's *Institutes of the Laws of England*: "For a man's house is his castle, *et domus sua cuique est tutissimum refugium* [and each man's home his safest refuge]" (*The Third Part of the Institutes of the Laws of England: Concerning High Treason and Other Pleas of the Crown and Criminal Causes* [London: E. and R. Brooke., 1797], 161).

32. "Rise and Rise Again: Making Ridley Scott's *Robin Hood*," Prod. Charles de Lauzirika (Lauzirika, 2010).

especially *Gladiator* (2000): a correlation Grazer clarifies when he states "I guess I've always felt like, if we made this movie. . . it would be kind of a *Gladiator* version of *Robin Hood*." Crowe himself similarly connects the two films, saying:

> Ridley and I have been very impatient since *Gladiator* because. . . every man and his dog wanted us to make *Gladiator 2* or another version of *Gladiator*. . . . And we've made three other films since then. And the funny thing is about them, you know, it doesn't matter what we do, everybody always compares them to *Gladiator*. Ridley very bravely at the beginning of the film said, you know, "Cut your hair exactly like it was at the beginning of *Gladiator*, and let's have your beard that way too." And I'm like, "Aw, man, people will just winge. . . ." And he said, "Look, if we're going to steal from anybody, we might as well steal from ourselves."

And steal from themselves they do in the film, with the chief exception of the ending. Though both Maximus and Robin gain wide popular appeal and work to advance democratic ideals for the people, in *Gladiator* Maximus ends up dead, crushed by the machine of imperial power, while Robin eludes royal power by escaping to the greenwood with Marian and friends where they live a democratic, bucolic life. This happy ending fulfills the film makers' version of the twelfth century: a space and time grounded in their imagination and self-justified sense of history. As Crowe notes, "We've tried to. . . redefine the times. . . in fact, shift the timeline: we kill Richard instead of having him ride in and save the day. . . but I think it's more historically accurate in my opinion, anyway, in terms of what, what the cultural milieu was that a Robin Hood character could arise out of."

Though through the film Crowe wants to realize Robin Hood's "cultural milieu," Grazer wants to imagine himself back into "a really brutal time," and Scott wants to "occupy that space" of twelfth-century England, they haven't really left the contemporary west. With its themes of ineffectual political leadership, over-taxation, the return home of the war-weary to an equally war-weary home-front population, and the backdrop of a conflicted middle east, the film echoes today's headlines, blogosphere, and editorial pages. It is also fundamentally an American story where difference doesn't exist beyond one's fashion, where any person with gumption can seize opportunities to advance socially and economically, and where ideas of personal liberty are paramount. This attention to contemporary issues and assumptions—cloaked though they are in twelfth-century garb—comes as no surprise, however, in light of screen writer Brian Helgeland's comments in the documentary on the making of the film. He says:

> My goal was to have all that entertainment and scope and scale from an historical film, but still have the audience say "I recognize that world in my own world" 'cause I don't think the world changes very much over time. People still fall in love, people still betray each other, people still have trouble paying the rent. And they have all that in Nottingham.

Nottingham is us; we are Nottingham: with one major exception beyond the obvious bits of dress, tools, and speech patterns. The proto-socialist, egalitarian greenwood fantasy with which the film ends, though lovely, sounds indeed legendary. The irony of the film's closing phrase—"And so the legend begins"—in the wake of the "greenwood fantasy-dream" I'm sure is unintentional given the earnestness with which Scott pursues his medieval imaginary in the rest of the film.

As with the film makers already discussed, Scott unknowingly strives for the same goal many nineteenth- and early twentieth-century scholars and artists sought: the "story behind the legend." In doing so he creates an ideal audience for the film that both accepts and celebrates the medieval world imagined: a world that sanctions the outlaw in the face of political tyranny. Not surprisingly, Scott's *Robin Hood* taps into the fundamental features of traditional British outlawry, which Stephanie L. Barczewski describes as "the separation drawn between legal and true justice, the notion that honest men turn to banditry only as a last resort, and, above all, the essentially patriotic character of the outlaw's actions."[33] Yet, viewed in light of American politics in 2010, Scott's harnessing of these features also taps—whether or not intentionally—into the fervor underlying current political discourse that expresses deep dissatisfaction with government. As he strives to "occupy that space" of twelfth-century England, Scott tells an origin story rooted in the *nostoi* tradition of the warrior returning home to chaos, in twentieth-century politics that sees government as tyrannical and opposition to it as just and patriotic, and in his own cinematic dreams, especially *Gladiator*.

---

33. Stephanie L. Barczewski, *Myth and National Identity in Nineteenth-Century Britain: The Legends of King Arthur and Robin Hood* (Oxford: Oxford UP, 2000), 41.

4. Conclusion

As with any work of art—classical sculpture, Renaissance painting, medieval cathedral, Baroque minuet, Anglo-Saxon epic, Old French romance, Middle English ballad—twenty-first century film is as much product of its own cultural milieu as it is "timeless" in any way. The four films discussed here suggest that part of the current cultural milieu these films both create and seek to satisfy is a desire for origins concerning legendary figures. In this desire, twenty-first century viewers and film makers are similar to nineteenth- and early twentieth-century scholars, artists, and their audiences. These earlier scholars and artists looked to the Middle Ages in part as a source for fostering nationalism. As Barczewski notes:

> In this period, the selective mobilization of the past—and the medieval past in particular—acted to overcome the tensions created in the present by the often tempestuous relationship among the nation's constituent communities. The Middle Ages could, if manipulated carefully, provide a portrait of a single nation with all its inhabitants marching together towards glory and greatness, rather than one of a hostile group of geographically proximate countries who were constantly warring against one another.[34]

Ernst Moritz Ludwig Ettmüller writing for a German-speaking audience, for instance, desired to link the oldest known epic in a Germanic language, *Beowulf*, to its Germanic origins in part to fuel his nationalist concerns.[35] And Lady Katie Magnus, writing for an English audience, argued "the seeds of our national character are to be sought in the lives of the heroes of early England, from whom we trace the beginnings of our best habits and institutions."[36]

Scholars and writers like Ettmüller and Magnus wish to see themselves in the past or at least to construct the past to argue for a particular future in which they imagine themselves. Again, the twenty-first century film makers discussed here do much the same thing. Just as the nineteenth- and early twentieth-century Arthur, for example, signals national unity in the face of an external threat, so does Fuqua's *King Arthur*, as its ending clearly shows. In this hoped-for future, realized through the

---

34. Barczewski, *Myth and National Identity*, 7.

35. Shippey, *Beowulf: The Critical Heritage*, 28-74.

36. Lady Katie Magnus, *First Makers of England: Julius Caesar, King Arthur, Alfred the Great* (London: John Murray, 1901), vii.

camera's imaginary telling of Arthur's origin, all Britons unite under the once-and-future king. While neither Gunnarsson nor Zemeckis is after Ettmüller's source texts, each desires and imaginatively fulfills the origin story of *Beowulf* by offering quintessentially twenty-first century tales. Telling a *bildungsroman*, Gunnarsson wants to celebrate diversity as his hero grows in sympathy for the other. Zemeckis, on the other hand, offers a morality tale with a simple lesson: avoid the corrupting temptations of sex, booze, and overweening pride. Both, in their efforts to tell true tales, undercut traditional Anglo-Saxon storytelling as they replace the poem's narrative with a cinematic translation of it. Scott like these others desires an origin story—the "untold" story of Robin Hood—and on the way he offers a reading of the outlaw that's much the same as earlier readings in which Robin signals the just opposition to oppressive tyranny. Though told in the trappings of twelfth-century England, Scott's film is of neither the rise of a king, nor a *bildungsroman*, nor even a morality tale; rather, it is a *nostos*, a return tale, in which an opportunist changes his clothes, adopts a new role, and turns underground political leader, poised to lead a revolt from his greenwood fantasyland. Like Fuqua, Gunnarsson, and Zemekis, Scott elides the fundamental alterity, or surprising otherness, of the Middle Ages to live in a "screen dream" that, like a Lacanian "day dream," cinematically fulfills a desire for origins by reflecting his own twenty-first century assumptions, predilections, and concerns.

The Arthurian Landscapes of Guy Gavriel Kay

M. J. Toswell, University of Western Ontario

GUY GAVRIEL KAY, A Canadian writer nowadays very well known in the world of fantasy fiction, plays particularly with European medieval moments and visionscapes.[1] His first novel, the high fantasy trilogy *The Fionavar Tapestry*, most obviously evokes Arthurian materials by having the three central figures of that legend (Arthur, Guinevere, and Lancelot) appear as well as Taliesin the bard. After this very traditional and highly Tolkienian work, Kay turned more and more to writing alternate history with steadily fewer and fewer magical elements and divine appearances. He also wrote largely single-volume works, setting one in a version of Renaissance Italy, the next in the Provence of the troubadours, then the Iberian Peninsula during the Reconquista, then Byzantium in its high medieval glory and intrigue (a two-part work), and finally Anglo-Saxon England in the time of king Alfred. His two most recent novels move yet further in the direction of alternate history with its elements of realism: *Ysabel* occurs in a modern setting with resonance from the Roman wars in Gaul, and *Under Heaven*, his most recent novel, tells part of the story of the Tang Dynasty in China. *Ysabel* is also the first of Kay's novels to interlink with a previous book obviously and explicitly, in that it reuses

---

1. Formal scholarship on Kay is somewhat limited, and to date most of the work on his writing appears in speculative fiction magazines and online fora. The website run with Kay's sanction by Deborah Meghnagi, http://www.brightweavings.com/ offers references to most of the available scholarship, both formal and informal; Kay's publishers have recently developed a somewhat more superficial website complete with the Penguin logo at the top of the main page. For a basic background see the entry by Holly E. Ordway, "Guy Gavriel Kay," in the *Dictionary of Literary Biography. Canadian Fantasy and Science-Fiction Writers*. Ed. Douglas Ivison. Vol. 251. (Detroit: Gale Group, 2002), 139–48; a less detailed version is Christine Mains, "Guy Gavriel Kay," in *Supernatural Fictional Writers: Contemporary Fantasy and Horror. Vol. II Guy Gavriel Kay to Roger Zelazny*. Ed. Richard Bleiler. (New York: Thomson Gale, 2003), 509–16.

The Arthurian Landscapes of Guy Gavriel Kay

two characters from the earlier *Fionavar Tapestry*.[2] Moreover, it picks up the Arthurian strand more obviously than his other novels, with a central trio of suffering and heroic individuals, a woman and two men who love her. I want to argue here that Kay's use of Arthurian materials is highly sophisticated, thoroughly intertextual, and highly literary. In particular, his approach to history is dense and interlayered, his settings and landscapes are stunning and carefully delineated, and his characters develop and change with great psychological consistency and human believability.

The Fionavar Tapestry is suffused with the matter of romance, to use the Frygian mode nowadays somewhat out of favour. It has what Gillian Beer terms the "highly stylized patterns," the strong connection to medieval literature with its adaptation of the Arthurian materials, and it has the central elements of a romance in Beer's terminology:

> The romance tends to use and re-use well-known stories whose familiarity reassures, and permits a subtly allusive presentation. Its remote sources are domesticated and brought close to present experience primarily because they are peopled with figures whose emotions and relationships are directly registered and described with profuse sensuous detail.[3]

Beer further argues that the romance "shows us the ideal" and because of that it is both escapist but also implicitly instructive, although it does have a tendency towards self-indulgence. Her closing description very aptly describes *The Fionavar Tapestry*, as she indicates that romance involves a "cluster of properties: the themes of love and adventure, a certain withdrawal from their own societies on the part of both reader and romance hero, profuse sensuous detail" and other elements of plot and character closing with "amplitude of proportions, a strongly enforced code of conduct to which all the characters must comply."[4] Fantasy novels, particularly high fantasy novels, follow this recipe with exactitude. Kay does so in his first trilogy and also does so, though with less precision, in *Ysabel*, the novel which won him the World Fantasy Award.

Neither Beer nor Northrop Frye himself offers a detailed discussion of the landscape of romance, though some points can be inferred. The

2. *Tigana* briefly references Kay's theory that all worlds are reflections of the originary world of Fionavar; Kay also reuses his construction of Christianity as the religion of Jad and various other religions.

3. Gillian Beer, *The Romance*. (London: Methuen, 1970), 2.

4. Beer, 10.

"sensuous details" that Beer adduces will be those details that mark the surroundings, flavour the actions, and bring the characters alive. Frye in *The Anatomy of Criticism* notes that the archetypal form of the romance is the quest and that generally the romance form involves a complete polarization of good and evil, the hero and the villain, with no subtlety of presentation.[5] Although Frye does not say it directly, the landscapes, too, ought to be archetypal: forests must be dark, dense and deadly to the ignorant, plains broad, open, and pitiless, cities anchored with castles and bustling with activity, the lair of evil in the north with huge vacant expanses of unlovely cold lands, and so forth. Frye's concern was with plot, theme and characterization, and he was less interested in other elements of literary texts.[6] His general statement on the matter is that the romance is a highly stylized mode. In fact, when in a later book he speaks more specifically about the romance, he contrasts the idyllic with the demonic modes and argues that the romance is an up-and-down mode in which the "world of ordinary experience" is replaced by a "dream world, in which the narrative movement keeps rising into wish fulfillment or sinking into anxiety and nightmare."[7] Kay's novel moves from earth to Fionavar—from a waking world to a dream possibility—and uses thereafter the five young Canadians as the focalizing figures who encounter the strangenesses and likenesses of the new world and engage with the joyous moments of accomplishment and horrifying moments of apocalyptic threat. *Ysabel* similarly focalizes through a naive narrator, a teen-aged Canadian boy in France, and alternates between the wholly grounded reality of modern Provence and the dreamlike irruption of three characters from late antiquity with supernatural qualities and pagan rites. The juxtaposition of the modern against the antique is genuinely disruptive and shocking.

History is, in fact, always dangerous for Kay. Its lessons are dark and ominous. Not to be ignored, it functions not as an additional character in the drama but as a dramatic situation that must be relived, step by step,

---

5. Northrop Frye, *The Anatomy of Criticism: Four Essays*. (Princeton: Princeton UP, 1957), 186–206. The discussion of the romance as a genre is pp. 303–26 when it is contrasted with the novel; here Frye proposes that the romance involves stylized figures who expand into psychological archetypes (304), and thereby is attracted to allegory.

6. For a similar use of Frye's approach see Tom Shippey, *J.R.R. Tolkien: Author of the Century*. (London: HarperCollins, 2001), 221–25.

7. Northrop Frye, *The Secular Scripture: A Study of the Structure of Romance*. (Cambridge, MA: Harvard UP, 1976), 53.

and in the process turned to another resolution. Not unlike the technique of directed dreaming, Kay's historical scapes force the characters through the exigencies of past plots in the hope that a different outcome can be achieved. Thus when the city-states of Italy are at war in *Tigana*, Kay finds a way, and intentionally a not-entirely-ethical way, to unite them against a common foe and achieve a lasting peace. The reconquest of Spain takes place in a matter of decades rather than over three bloody centuries, and the final battle is a duel between two friends who are the chosen champions of the two religions, the two kingdoms, after which a permanent peace establishes itself. This desire to find new outcomes is presaged by *The Fionavar Tapestry*, although in that case it is a legend which Kay chooses to reconfigure leading to a new and thoroughly romantic outcome—in the Northrop Frye sense of the word. He takes the legend of King Arthur as perpetually returning and has the quintet of central characters recall the king from the dead as penance for an episode early in his reign. When he learned that a child would grow up to become Mordred and would bring down his kingdom, Arthur slaughtered all the children born in that area during May.[8] As a result, according to Kay, he does not enjoy perpetual peace, but must come alive when called by someone with the correct term, *Childslayer*. Kim, the seer who is the heart of the five Canadians called to Fionavar, learns his name from his father, buried at Stonehenge. Another of the quintet, Jennifer, emerges as the reborn Guinevere, and Arthur himself chooses, late in the second volume of the trilogy, to call Lancelot back from the dead in Cader Sedat. The Celtic underpinnings of the Arthurian material link together with Malory's version here, so that Arthur and Guinevere are solidly established before the advent of Lancelot to destabilize both their love and their kingdom—and at the same time, ironically, to lift the kingdom and the ethical conflict of individual choice against public good to new heights. In Kay's version, Guinevere sends Lancelot upon impossible quests, one of which he unsurprisingly accomplishes only by tainting his own sense of honor (a motif originating with Chretien de Troyes but followed by several Arthurian writers including Malory). At the end of the novel, Kay offers redemption to all three central characters, and to Cafall the dog, in a climactic and thoroughly fantastic scene in which they are permitted to move on together and without further conflict to a paradisiacal afterlife. Kay likes to tie his

---

8. This is the last section of Book I of Malory. See *Malory: Works*, ed. E. Vinaver. (London: Oxford UP, 1971), 37.

historical legends in tightly, so he has a Taliesin figure, reference to how Gawain battled Lancelot unfairly and even tried to blind him in a duel by manoeuvring him so that the sun is in his eyes (thereby taking unfair advantage), and an episode corresponding exactly to the story of Elaine, the lady who dies of unrequited love for Lancelot. Finally, Kay even has a complicated son-figure, this time of Guinevere, who has the opportunity to damn or to redeem all of Fionavar. In defence of that son Lancelot commits his dishonourable act:

> In the instant before the demon was upon him he turned to Darien. Flidais saw their eyes lock and hold. Then he heard Lancelot say quickly, in a voice drained of all inflection, "One final cast, in memory of Gawain. I have nothing left. *Count ten for me, then scream. And then pray to whatever you like.*"
>
> He had time for no more. Sidestepping with a half-spin, he launched himself in another rolling dive away from the murderous hammer. It smote the ground where he had stood, and Flidais flinched back from the thunder of that stroke and the heat that roared up from the riven ground.[9]

Some few seconds later, Lancelot uses the distraction that Darien provides to carve off the hammer formed from the demon's own shape-shifting body and somehow lifts and throws it "with all the passion of an unmatched soul" to kill the oldest of all the forest-demons. And a few minutes later, he begs Flidais/Taliesin never to speak of the incident because of his shame; he sought aid in single combat. His code is very precise; because Guinevere asked him to help the boy, he did. And he explicitly tells Darien that he has been freed "to follow your road." That quest Lancelot can aid in, but he cannot follow it himself; in other words, this is a typical Maloryean moment as played through Tennyson. The absolute rigidity of the code that Lancelot, Guinevere, and Arthur chain themselves to willingly is something that Kay wants to admire and extol, but also to subvert and question. In this respect he is certainly a writer at the cusp of the twenty-first century.

A similar sensibility affects Kay's approach to Provence, with its blood-soaked history contrasted against its stunning natural beauty and remarkable Roman edifications. Here, too, Kay has the Guinevere figure develop from one of the modern characters and become a Celtic warrior princess, but with the contemporary sensibility of a photographer's

---

9. *The Fionavar Tapestry*, 619 and 621.

managing assistant. The male figures of the trio materialize offstage; one of them is a massive bearded and hirsute Celtic warrior (probably more Saxon than Celtic) who has over the centuries learned to shapeshift and to develop some magical abilities, and the other is a lithe small whippet of a Roman with the brutally short hair of a career military man, great cleverness, and ability at manipulating and reading others. Both are ruthless warriors who want to duel each other, the winner to achieve the lady and the loser to die in the battle or as a mercy thereafter. Here, too, Kay uses the notion of the unexpected child to create a situation in which the centuries-old conflict between the two men over the woman must be resolved, in this case and somewhat more brutally with the death of both men at the site of an ancient massacre. The woman, Ysabel, returns to her modern self as Melanie, though eternally changed by her experience, and the boy who has served as catalyst for the resolution has the chance to return to being a normal teenager (if that is possible). History is very much more present here than in the high fantasy trilogy, and much more brutal. Given that Fionavar is battling a god, the actual violence is interestingly limited to specific moments, whereas the irruption of violence is both quite frequent and quite shocking when it charges into the very ordinary everyday life of a Canadian teenager in Provence for the summer with his photographer father and the assistants who set up his shots. That violence is embedded in quite specific historical incidents and evoked by encounters with the monuments and with individuals. Thus, when the quest for Ysabel (Melanie) has begun, followed by the Celt, the Roman, and also by the modern figures who want to reclaim their friend, the Celt engages in a philosophical discussion with the teenager at Glanum over the way in which history was changed when Ysabel first gave the cup to the Roman at a feast:

> Cadell was looking at the pool again. Glanis, water-goddess. The water looked dark, unhealthy. The Celt's large hands were loosely clasped. In profile, composed and seemingly at ease, he no longer seemed the flamboyant, violent figure of before.
>
> As if to mock that thought, he looked up at Ned again. "I killed him here once, twenty steps behind you. I cut off his head after, with an axe, spitted it on a spike. Left it in front of one of their temples."[10]

---

10. *Ysabel*, 304–5.

The characters in a Kay novel are well aware of the complexities and incongruities of their roles in history and of how choices that they make may change history. They are also completely embedded in their settings, aware that how they interact with their environment can also change the course of history. The courtly love trios in particular have changed and shifted over Kay's novels, gaining in complexity and individuality. The straightforward retelling of Arthurian legend in *The Fionavar Tapestry* is complicated only slightly by the hints of an earlier such doomed courtly love trio, with the tale of Galadan, Amairgen, and Lisen serving as a kind of pessimistic background which gives Galadan the right to be embittered and evil, the lieutenant of the dark Lord. In *A Song for Arbonne*, the other novel Kay sets in Provence, a courtly love trio is the core of the tale, manipulated into cooperating to produce the correct ending in which the poets of Arbonne successfully repulse the violent fascists of Gorhaut who attempt to take over their land.

Kay's settings tend to be, as a direct consequence of their importance in his novels, sumptuous and highly detailed. Like Ursula LeGuin, he takes a profoundly anthropological approach to his settings, so that when Dave Martyniuk finds himself in the plains in Fionavar, he immerses himself in a culture with spirit-quests, a profound sense of the importance of the tribe, and a deep love for the animals which provide the sustenance for their existence—the flights of eltor. The details of life on the plains are lovingly described and also incorporated into the plot and into the way in which the men of the plains debate amongst themselves and fight for Fionavar. Similarly the Tolkienian dwarves under the mountain, conflicted and somewhat uncertain in their loyalties to good or evil, inhabit carved and lofty corridors and have as their central symbol and the keeper of their conscience and rule, a crystal dragon studded with colours like precious gems:

> Then it spread its wings, and Kimberly cried aloud in wonder and awe, for the wings of the Dragon dazzled and shone with a myriad of colours like gems in infinite variety, a play of light in the meadow bowl of night. She almost did sink to her knees then, but again something kept her on her feet, watching, her heart aching.
>
> The Dragon did not fly. It held itself suspended, half within the water, half rising from it. Then it opened its mouth, and flame burst forth, flame without smoke, like the torches on the walls

within the mountain; blue-white flame, through which the stars could still be seen.[11]

The symbol of the dwarves, the dragon in Calor Diman, the mountain pool beneath the stars, ties directly to the dwarves and their production of light in their halls. The dragon also ties directly to its role in the fight of good against evil and even reflects the sheer height and clarity of vision possible given the altitude of the mountain of the dwarves. It is also, rather obviously, a creature of high fantasy, and the exuberant description contains the kind of verbal arabesques and poetic imagery that such creatures require in this genre.

Descriptions of mountains in later works such as *Ysabel* can be equally imposing and impressive, but they link to the supernatural world only through the activities of the humans forced to relive the history of the place. On two occasions the fifteen-year-old Ned Marriner comes close to Mont Sainte-Victoire, the central symbol and plot place of the novel. The first time he is with his father's assistants as they search for a good photographic image:

> Ned was impressed. Hard not to be. Seen this close, Mont Sainte-Victoire completely dominated the landscape. It wasn't huge, you weren't going to skateboard down it in winter or anything, but there were no other mountains or hills around and the triangular peak was crisp and imposing. At the very top Ned saw a white cross. . . .
> . . .The stony bleakness above the green meadow didn't say 'pretty' to him. It felt more powerful and unsettling than that. He was going to say something, but in the minute or so since they'd stopped and gotten out he had started to feel peculiar. He kept his mouth shut. Steve took a few more digitals.[12]

The description is terse, in no way florid, and framed carefully through the point of view of a teenager. Moreover, the description of the mountain folds directly into Ned's reaction to it. Some minutes later he is seeing through a red haze of blood, an evocation of the genocide perpetrated by the victorious Romans upon the massed families of the Celts they defeated in late antiquity. This mountain runs in the blood of the boy and marks him with its suffering. Later in the novel, he runs up the

11. *The Fionavar Tapestry*, 680.
12. *Ysabel*, 74–5.

mountain to find Ysabel at the garagai, the site of the slaughter, and end the centuries-old triangle of love and death:

> He was in a darkened space, not too large, sheltered from the wind, level underfoot. A rock roof disappeared into shadow above. He didn't know what he'd expected to see, but he didn't see anything.
>
> He turned to look south and his jaw dropped at the wonder of it, the quiet beauty spread out through that wider opening, as if it were a window onto glory. The fields below, a glinting line of river, the land rising a very little, and falling, and then rising again across the river towards mountains in the distance, shining in the late, clear light, and then the far blue of the sea.[13]

The description remains spare and crisp here, and the focus has turned from the mountain itself to the land it overlooks and protects. Once he has achieved his goal of reaching the garagai, Ned's perception of the southern lands, the lands of Provence, offers a "glinting line" of hope that the history of the place might alter from blood-soaked to peaceful, from being tied into an age-old triangle of mutual love and misery to achieving a close. This is, after all, a fantasy novel, and achieving closure remains possible and even probable.

As will already be clear, the history and settings of Kay's novels bind themselves very tightly into the character development and the decisions the individual characters make. Although the climax of *The Fionavar Tapestry* comes when the boy Darien chooses for the Light, the forces of good, and kills the evil god who is his father, the turning point comes slightly earlier in the novel, when the younger prince of Fionavar, Diarmuid, chooses the single combat that should go to Arthur, or failing him to Lancelot. He duels a monstrous and augmented urgach (a very much larger orc) on a six-legged slaug, and although he manages to kill the monstrous leader of the forces of evil, he dies himself in order to accomplish the feat:

> And then, as white pain exploded within him in the darkness, towering, indescribable, as his life's blood fountained to fall among the stones, Diarmuid dan Ailell, with the last strength of his soul, almost the very last of his self-control, with Sharra's face before him, not Uathach's, did the final deed of his days. He rose up above his agony, and with his left hand he clutched the hairy arm that held the black sword, and with his right, pulling himself forward,

---

13. *Ysabel*, 471.

as towards a long-sought dream of overwhelming Light, he thrust his own bright blade into the urgach's face and out the back of its head, and he killed it in Andarien, just after the sun had set.[14]

Diarmuid is a scintillant character throughout the novel, a younger son who appears to be a ne'er-do-well, enjoys drinking and wenching in the low-class taverns in the city rather than the more refined activities of the court, and was as a child ignored more or less completely by a father obsessed by the excellencies of his first-born. At the same time, he is the principal driver of the plot, creating situations and resolving them in ways that help the side of Light more than the activities of his elder and more accomplished brother. He objects explicitly when Arthur chooses to bring Lancelot to life in Fionavar, saying that this is neither wanted nor required, and his actions, while offering comic relief, also bring all the characters together to the last confrontation with the forces of evil. He is the classic ignored younger son who chooses to retaliate by ignoring the conventions of his society in favour of making his own way; Kay rather delights in providing him with clever quips, a band of warriors in the Robin Hood tradition of personal loyalty, total success with women and at hunting, and a secret but absolute code of honour. His sacrifice at this point in the novel, wholly unexpected from the reader's point of view but wholly predictable once it has occurred, marks the point at which the characters genuinely recognise that free will is paramount. As a result of his choice, the Arthurian triangle has its opportunity for redemption and resolution.

The character development in *Ysabel* is similarly imbricated with the plot. Throughout the novel, Ned has been running and keeping a journal for his coach. The running has brought him to some adventures and has also become a way for him to become more real in Provence, more connected to the land than the usual passing tourist. In the final pages of the novel, it becomes clear that the only way to find Ysabel (with Melanie subsumed inside the Celtic princess) is to run up Mont Sainte-Victoire at dusk, and to get there before the two warriors. Ned is the only one of the contingent who could accomplish the feat, and he is also the right person to do it. Nonetheless, in the world of heroic exploits, running up a switchback path does not seem a major accomplishment. The veteran warrior Dave Martyniuk, or the sisters Meghan and Kim, or even the

---

14. *The Fionavar Tapestry*, 707.

father who has earlier made it clear that he would die to protect his son, or even the other two assistants of Edward Marriner: all these might seem more appropriate choices for the final confrontation. But Kay has built the whole novel circling around the mountain and its garagai, and circling around the knowledge that Melanie would have had to deploy in her own behalf, and circling around the teenager growing into his powers and his knowledge—and here using the talent that has been his for some years. So Ned heads out, not to fight, but simply to be present, a wild card at the confrontation of the two men with the woman:

> He wiped sweat off his forehead with the back of one hand. She was up there. He knew it as surely as he'd known anything. And there was only him here, Ned Marriner. Not his aunt—whatever she'd done once, she couldn't do it now. Neither could his uncle. His mom could treat refugees in the Sudan but she couldn't get up this mountain in time or do anything at the top if she did. Ned was the one linked to all this, seeing the blood, smelling the memory of bloodshed.
>
> You didn't *ask* for the roles you were given in life; not always, anyhow.
>
> He realized that he was clenching his jaw. He made himself relax. You couldn't run that way, and he had running to do. He swung his pack off, fished his iPod out and put the buds in his ears. He dialed up Coldplay. Maybe rock would do what bracelets and rowan leaves couldn't.[15]

Kay focalizes through Ned, and offers Ned's actual thoughts as he figures out a way to go forward and strategizes about how to reduce his reaction to the violent battle that took place there. His choice of Coldplay might seem unusual, but his knowledge about the relaxation he needs to run and his ruminations about the role he is playing here are both believable and substantial steps forward by comparison with the young boy of several days earlier at the beginning of the novel. The echoes of history and folklore reflected by the vellin bracelet given by his Aunt Kim, and the rowan leaves proffered by Vera, and the complex psychological reflections of the ways in which his own contribution to moral goodness might or might not reach the level of his mother's good works: they add resonance to Ned's thinking and strengthen the sense of him as a fully-drawn character.

15. *Ysabel*, 459.

Significant differences between the two novels also require attention. Whereas *The Fionavar Tapestry* builds a huge canvas and engages in several quests—through the forest, over the sea, across the plains, and crucially far into the northlands—the more recent novel fixes itself with one main plot, albeit a complex one. The Arthurian elements are integral to both, but where they are explicit and almost disruptive for the reader in the first work, they are implicit and have to be inferred and thought through afterwards in the second. That is, Kay obliges the reader to have the true double vision of a complex readerly engagement with the material by retelling the story of Arthur, Lancelot and Guinevere complete with Fionavar versions of well-known sub-tales, and insists on bringing about a somewhat awkward happy ending. The landscapes are pure romance, the history a clear recreation of Malory's text for the discerning reader (and with enough hints added in for readers not aware of all the details of the Arthurian material), and the characters explicitly have the motivations—to the point of being quite stylized and even perhaps allegorical—of their Arthurian forebears. In *Ysabel* the landscape is considerably more precise and realistic, described in spare prose and hinting at the glories of a summer in Provence rather than describing them all in sensuous detail; the story is at once new and old since the characters describe it themselves as an age-old human story in which they are caught and doomed to repetition, and the characters grow and change throughout. The reader might well suspect that the Celtic character is Arthur and the Frankish/Roman stranger is Lancelot, but these are allusions overlaying otherwise fully-developed characters, albeit romance characters. In other words, Kay has changed his approach to his romances and altered the sensuousness of his language, but not his romance plots or characters.

Kay argues himself in a recent paper that fantasy is often pigeon-holed in the category of "fiction-as-distraction," but it has the capacity to be both powerful and important. Notably, he suggests, "Fantasy can also be a way of dealing with history, with the elements of our own past."[16] Kay believes that fantasy-writing allows him to introduce moral issues from the past and address them anew. Notably he uses mythic figures from the past in confrontation with figures who share modern sensibilities. In so doing he highlights the conflicts and reaches for the possibility of finding

---

16. See Guy Gavriel Kay, "The Fiction of Privacy: Fantasy and the Past," *Journal of the Fantastic in the Arts*. 20.2 (2009), 240–9. Essentially the same article appears earlier in "Privacy and the Ethics of Literature," *Queen's Quarterly* 108.1 (2001), 46–55.

a new way of resolving them; his novels reclaim not history but the philosophical or moral issues of history. Diarmuid and Ned both serve as Galahad figures, offering themselves as the sacrifice that can permit new modes of being and different choices from the central Arthurian trio in the romance settings of these novels. They oblige the reader to rethink both the structure of the novel and the choices of its characters; in such reconsideration does Kay's reason for writing lie. Lynne Truss argues in a recent book that:

> It is now pretty well established that the human brain needs to think about something beyond itself—something fairly complex and open-ended, ideally involving lots of characters who need to be kept straight in one's head, and regular exciting landmark events. On the one hand, *The Archers* evolved to fill this need–and, on the other hand, so did sport.[17]

Probably Truss was no more aware of the way in which her formula describes what I would nowadays call "big fantasy" than was Northrop Frye in an earlier generation. But, of course, it does. The landscape of the one might be the football pitch or the cricket ground and of the other an equally stylized medieval walled city or a frightening forest or an uncharted sea, but both are the landscapes of romance.

---

17. Lynne Truss, *Get Her Off the Pitch! How Sport took over my life*. (London: Fourth Estate, 2009), 104. Truss is more famous for her books on punctuation and etiquette, and possibly for her work as a comic, but for some years she wrote a column for *The Times* sports pages entitled "Kicking and Screaming" and involving her reactions to a whole series of sports she had never before encountered. This book is her more reasoned later reaction to the experience.

www.ingramcontent.com/pod-product-compliance
Lightning Source LLC
Chambersburg PA
CBHW070522090426
42735CB00012B/2855